SPIRITUAL GIFTS

A Practical Guide to How God Works Through You

David Francis

LifeWay Press®
Nashville, Tennessee

ISBN 978-0-6330-9936-7 • Item 001220730

Dewey decimal classification: 234.13
Subject heading: SPIRITUAL GIFTS

Unless indicated otherwise, Scripture quotations are taken from the Holman
Christian Standard Bible®, Copyright © 1999, 2000, 2002, 2003, 2009 by
Holman Bible Publishers. Used by permission. Holman Christian Standard
Bible® and HCSB® are federally registered trademarks of Holman Bible
Publishers. Scripture quotations marked NIV are taken from the Holy Bible,
NEW INTERNATIONAL VERSION®. Copyright © 1973, 1978, 1984 by
Biblica Inc. All rights reserved worldwide. Used by permission. Scripture
quotations marked KJV are taken from the King James Version of the Bible.
Scripture quotations marked NASB are taken from the New American
Standard Bible®, Copyright © 1960, 1962, 1963, 1968, 1971, 1972, 1973,
1975, 1977, 1995 by The Lockman Foundation. Used by permission.
(lockman.org) Scripture quotations marked TLB are taken from
The Living Bible, copyright ©1971. Used by permission of Tyndale
House Publishers Inc., Wheaton, IL 60189 USA. All rights reserved.

To order additional copies of this resource, write to LifeWay Resources
Customer Service; One LifeWay Plaza; Nashville, TN 37234;
order online at LifeWay.com; email orderentry@lifeway.com;
phone toll free 800-458-2772; fax 615-251-5933;
or visit the LifeWay Christian Store serving you.

Printed in the United States of America

Groups Ministry Publishing • LifeWay Resources
One LifeWay Plaza • Nashville, TN 37234

CONTENTS

ACKNOWLEDGMENTS / THE AUTHOR

This material would never have been developed except for the encouragement of my predecessor as minister of education at First Baptist Garland, Dr. Carr Suter, who served the church in that capacity for almost three decades. I will always cherish the years I served as minister with adults under his gifted leadership.

Loving thanks to my wife, Vickie, who let a lot of chores go undone during the many weekends I spent revising the material.

Special thanks to the many gifted folks at LifeWay who made this study a reality. Thanks to Henry Webb and J. J. Goldman for their prodding and encouragement to tackle the task. Thanks to the gifted editorial and design team that refined it. Marvin Owen, Chris Johnson, and Judi Hayes are encouraging, gifted editors. There are dozens of other gifted folks behind the scenes who have made this study possible. I am deeply grateful for their contributions.

David Francis

David Francis originally developed this material in 1988 while on the education staff of First Baptist Church, Garland, Texas, where he served for 13 years before joining LifeWay in 1997. David and his wife, Vickie, love teaching preschoolers on Sunday mornings and connecting with adults in their church in Hendersonville, Tennessee.

An Introduction to Spiritual Gifts

This week you will—
- learn that understanding spiritual gifts is a biblical mandate;
- identify the spiritual gifts in the four key passages that list them;
- match the names of 17 gifts with a brief definition;
- discover how a church where all members exercise their spiritual gifts presents a complete picture of Jesus to its community;
- define what a spiritual gift is and what it is not;
- understand some rewards of discovering your spiritual gift(s);
- understand some roadblocks that could keep you from experiencing the full joy of your spiritual gift(s).

Key Bible Passages
Four key passages in the Bible address the doctrine of spiritual gifts. Read each passage in its entirety before you begin this important study. Jot down any questions that come to mind as you read. Hopefully, most of them will be answered in the course of this study. These four key passages are 1 Peter 4:9-11; Romans 12:1-16; 1 Corinthians 12:1–14:30; and Ephesians 4:1-16.

"Are You Trying to Trick Me into Taking a Church Job?"
Teaching and preaching about spiritual gifts has often been used as a platform to communicate, "We have a lot of vacant positions in our church ministries, so get with it and fill one of them." That is not the motive behind this study! You may seek a new way to serve in your church as a result of this study, but that is not its primary goal. And you may complete this study with renewed energy and joy in your current role, but that's not the main point either.

My prayer is that your study of this material will help you to—
- experience Jesus in a fresh way as you see Him at work through each of the spiritual gifts;
- appreciate the genius of how Jesus designed the church as His new body, continuing every aspect of His earthly ministry through the spiritual gifts;
- understand the joy of allowing Jesus to minister through you as you exercise the spiritual gifts He has given you.

This Week's Key Verse
Based on the gift they have received, everyone should use it to serve others, as good managers of the varied grace of God (1 Pet. 4:10).

This Week's Lessons
Day 1: Getting Fired Up About Spiritual Gifts

Day 2: Making a List, Checking It Twice

Day 3: A Complete Picture of Jesus

Day 4: Spiritual Gifts Defined

Day 5: Rewards and Roadblocks

Key Bible Passages
✠ 1 Peter 4:9-11

✠ Romans 12:1-16

✠ 1 Corinthians 12:1–14:40

✠ Ephesians 4:1-16

Note: See pages 5–6 for more information about spiritual gifts inventories.

DAY 1

Getting Fired Up About Spiritual Gifts

Is it really that important to understand the doctrine of spiritual gifts? Let's see what the Bible says about that.

Read these Scriptures; then answer the question below.
- 1 Timothy 4:14a,15
- 2 Timothy 1:6
- 1 Corinthians 12:1

According to these verses, would you say that understanding about spiritual gifts is:
❑ optional for the Christian or
❑ commanded by scripture?

Through the apostle Paul, God commands Christians to understand spiritual gifts.

Timothy knew about spiritual gifts. In the first of his two letters to this young minister, Paul cautioned Timothy against neglecting the spiritual gift he had received. Perhaps Timothy was experiencing a case of burn out. In his second letter Paul reminded Timothy that his gift was still alive. Paul employed the imagery of a smoldering fire. Imagine a late-night campfire or fireplace after the flames have died away. The embers are still glowing. Paul encouraged Timothy to "keep ablaze" the gifts God had given him. Other translations render the command "stir up" (KJV), "fan into flame" (NIV), or "kindle afresh" (NASB). My pastor, David Landrith, encourages us to "stay fired up!" If you are a Christian, you have at least one spiritual gift that God wants you to "fire up" in service to Him!

The word translated *ignorant* can also be rendered *unaware* (HCSB, NASB). In the original Greek, it is a form of the word *agnosis,* from which we get the English word *agnostic.* Unlike an atheist, who does not believe God exists, an agnostic simply disregards God's activity in his life. Paul cautions against being an *agnostic* when it comes to spiritual gifts!

Do not neglect the gift that is in you. ... Practice these things; be committed to them, so that your progress may be evident to all (1 Tim. 4:14-15).

Keep ablaze the gift of God that is in you (2 Tim. 1:6).

Now about spiritual gifts ... I do not want you to be ignorant (1 Cor. 12:1, NIV).

This word can also be translated "misinformed" (Amplified Version). That was the big problem in the church at Corinth. At least one influential group in that church apparently thought they had a clear understanding about gifts. In fact, they were proud of their understanding. Paul wrote them primarily to correct their misunderstanding. Some in the church felt they were more spiritual than others because they exhibited certain gifts. They exercised their gifts in such a way as to draw attention to themselves. As Paul gently corrected these spiritual showoffs, he wrote, "Now to each one the manifestation of the Spirit is given for the common good" (1 Cor. 12:7, NIV).

According to this verse, which of the following is most true?
❑ God gifts some special people in the church for their own good.
❑ God gifts all people in the church for their own good.
❑ God gifts every believer for the good of the entire church.

The moment you received Jesus Christ as your Lord and Savior, the Holy Spirit took up residence in your life. Every believer is gifted by the Spirit. This not for his or her sake alone, but for the good of all. The word translated "common good" is the Greek *sympheron,* from which we get the English word *symphony.*

Think about that picture as you consider these verses:
• Romans 12:4-5
• Ephesians 4:16

In God's "kingdom symphony," who is important? _____
_____

Each one, performing his or her assigned part, is important in God's kingdom! Most choral music has at least four parts: soprano, alto, tenor, and bass (SATB). More difficult pieces might have additional parts (SSAATTBB, for example) and are usually only tackled by larger choirs. When I directed a church choir while stationed on an Air Force base on a mid-Atlantic island, we only had 14 voices and thought it a grand accomplishment to sing an anthem with three-part harmony (SAB).

How many "parts" are there when it comes to spiritual gifts? What "part" has God assigned to you? During the next couple of days, we will explore the lists of gifts in the New Testament to help answer those questions. All the lists come from the letters of Paul

As we have many parts in one body, and all the parts do not have the same function, in the same way we who are many are one body in Christ and individually members of one another (Rom. 12:4-5).

From Him the whole body, fitted and knit together by every supporting ligament, promotes the growth of the body for building up itself in love by the proper working of each individual part (Eph. 4:16).

except one, which was written by the apostle Peter. If Peter's letters were the only portion of God's Word you had, you might conclude that there are only three "parts."

See if you can find the three gifts the apostle Peter mentions in 1 Peter 4:9-11. List them here.

Hospitality
Service
Speaking

In verse 11, Peter distinguished between speaking gifts and serving gifts. In verse 9 Peter identified the need for the gift of hospitality.

Suppose these three categories of gifts were the only ones in the Bible. At this early point in our study, which one do you think best describes you?

❑ **Speaking.** Check here if you are most fulfilled when you are communicating (including talking, of course, but also writing, singing, drama, etc.).

❑ **Serving.** Check here if you prefer planning, working, doing, and accomplishing things, perhaps even behind the scenes.

❑ **Hospitality.** Check here if you feel compelled to reach out to others—even strangers—making them feel welcome and inviting them to God's house—or yours!

If you checked at least one of the boxes above, congratulations! You are a gifted person! Maybe you are a new Christian and are just being introduced to spiritual gifts. Perhaps you have been a Christian for a long time and have a desire to discover your gift or be more certain about it. Maybe you just need to rekindle your spiritual life and get fired up again. Wherever you are on your spiritual journey, this study will help you.

Be hospitable to one another without complaining. Based on the gift they have received, everyone should use it to serve others, as good managers of the varied grace of God. If anyone speaks, his speech should be like the oracles of God; if anyone serves, his service should be from the strength God provides, so that in everything God may be glorified through Jesus Christ. To Him belong the glory and the power forever and ever. Amen (1 Pet. 4:9-11).

DAY 2

Making a List,
Checking It Twice

No one biblical passage offers a complete, comprehensive list of the spiritual gifts. Peter identified speaking, serving, and hospitality. The apostle Paul wrote about gifts in his letters to the churches at Rome, Corinth, and Ephesus. Compare what he said to each church.

Paul's shortest list of gifts is found in Ephesians 4:11.

List those four gifts:
A postles
P rophets
E vangelist
P astors **and T** eachers

He personally gave some to be apostles, some prophets, some evangelists, some pastors and teachers (Eph. 4:11).

Some biblical scholars argue that the need for—and thus the gifts of—apostles and prophets expired with the completion of God's written Word, the Bible. It is outside the scope of this brief study to deal with that issue in detail. We will talk a little more about apostles in week 2. We will use the term *apostleship* to refer to the modern-day expression of the first-century gift of apostle. Paul identified the gift of *prophecy* in another passage, so we will use that term to describe those today who share traits similar to those of prophets of the biblical era.

The gifts of evangelist and pastor-teacher are also found only here. This has led some to conclude that these four gifts fall into a special category, reserved primarily for the clergy. For the purpose of this study, we will assume that God distributes these gifts to lay ministers as well as called/vocational ministers. Some laypersons are uncomfortable identifying themselves with the terms *evangelist* and *pastor*, which they associate with vocational ministers. So to avoid getting sidetracked, we will use the terms *evangelism* and *shepherding* to identify these gifts.

How do we get from *pastor* to *shepherding*? In early Latin translations of the New Testament, the Greek word *poimen* was rendered *pastores*. That's where we got the English word *pastor*.

These words are more accurately translated *shepherd*. This gift is not restricted to vocational pastors. In fact, your pastor might not have the gift of shepherding at all. Even if he does, he needs lots of assistant shepherds to meet the needs of all the sheep in the church flock.

Paul lists seven more gifts in Romans 12:6-8.

Use the passage to complete the names of the gifts below.

P _ _ _ _ _ _ cy
S _ _ _ ice
T _ _ _ _ ing
E _ _ _ _ _ _ ing
G _ _ _ _ _ g
L _ _ _ ing
M _ _ _ _

According to the grace given to us, we have different gifts: If prophecy, use it according to the standard of faith; if service, in service; if teaching, in teaching; if exhorting, in exhortation; giving, with generosity; leading, with diligence; showing mercy, with cheerfulness (Rom. 12:6-8).

These words appear in various translations with slight differences. So that we will all be talking about the same thing during this study, we will use these terms: *prophecy, service* (translated "ministry" in the KJV, "serving" in others), *exhortation* (the NIV has "encouraging") *teaching, giving* ("contributing" in the NIV), *leadership* ("ruling" in the KJV, "leading" in others), and showing *mercy*.

Paul included two lists when he wrote the Corinthian church. The first list appears in 1 Corinthians 12.

Look first at verses 8-10 and list only the gifts not already identified.

W _ _ _ _ _ _
K _ _ _ _ _ _ _ _ _
F _ _ _ _
H _ _ _ _ _ _ _ s
M _ _ _ _ _ _ _ _
D _ _ _ _ _ _ _ _ _ _ _ _ _ ing between spirits
L _ _ _ _ _ _ _ _ _
I _ _ _ _ _ _ _ _ _ _ _ _ _ _ of languages

To one is given a message of wisdom through the Spirit, to another, a message of knowledge by the same Spirit, to another, faith by the same Spirit, to another, gifts of healing by the one Spirit, to another, the performing of miracles, to another, prophecy, to another, distinguishing between spirits, to another, different kinds of languages, to another, interpretation of languages (1 Cor. 12:8-10).

Of the nine gifts in this passage, all but prophecy are found only in this list. Some of the Corinthians thought wisdom, knowledge, faith, healings, miracles, distinguishing between spirits, languages, and interpretation of languages were the best gifts. They thought these sign gifts distinguished those who were really spiritual from those who were not. Paul's primary purpose in 1 Corinthians 12–14 is to correct that notion.

Although he affirmed these gifts, Paul strongly asserted that they are no more important, and perhaps even less important, than the less spectacular gifts. These gifts have triggered more than their share of heated discussion and hurtful division within the body of Christ. This is doubly true of the gifts of tongues (languages), interpretation, healings, and miracles. We will explore these gifts again in week 5.

Because of the controversial nature of the four gifts just mentioned, we will emphasize only the gifts of *wisdom, knowledge, faith,* and *discernment.* Further, we will assume that none of these gifts is any believer's primary gift. By the time we get to week 5, you will probably already have a pretty good idea about what your primary spiritual gift might be. You'll then be ready to discover how these gifts sometimes serve to supplement the other spiritual gifts within the body of Christ.

Now look at 1 Corinthians 12:28-31.

List only the two gifts that have not already been identified above. List them here:

H __ __ ping
M __ __ __ __ ing

Some writers equate the gifts of *helping* (or helps) and *managing* ("administration" in the NIV; "governments" in the KJV) with the gifts of service and leadership in Romans 12. The Greek words are different, however, so we will treat them as two separate gifts. Although helping and service, managing and leadership have similarities, they also have distinct characteristics. We will study all four in more detail in week 2. To be consistent with most gift inventories, we will use the terms *helps* and *administration* to identify these gifts.

Are there other spiritual gifts? Some teachers include the gift of celibacy (or singleness), citing 1 Corinthians 7:1-9, and/or martyr, citing 1 Corinthians 13:3. Having acknowledged these two gifts, we will not explore them in detail.

God has placed these in the church: first apostles, second prophets, third teachers, next, miracles, then gifts of healing, helping, managing, various kinds of languages. Are all apostles? Are all prophets? Are all teachers? Do all do miracles? Do all have gifts of healing? Do all speak in languages? Do all interpret? But desire the greater gifts. And I will show you an even better way (1 Cor. 12:28-31).

As to the larger question—Are there other spiritual gifts?—there are two basic positions. Check the one below that seems to make the most sense to you at this point in our study. Neither answer is wrong!

❑ Since each list differs, Paul intended the lists to be illustrative rather than comprehensive. Therefore, there may be other gifts.

❑ Whether aware of God's inspiration or not, Peter and Paul were writing Scripture. Therefore, taken together, the gifts named in the New Testament make up a complete, and closed, list.

Review the key verse for this week. Ask God to reveal your spiritual gifts to you. Pledge to use your gifts to serve others.

In the space below, write a prayer to God about your spiritual gifts.

_____

_____

_____

_____

_____

_____

_____

_____

_____

_____

_____

_____

_____

DAY 3

A Complete Picture of Jesus

When Jesus of Nazareth walked on our planet, He was fully equipped with every spiritual gift. During His earthly ministry, Jesus demonstrated that He possessed the full range of spiritual giftedness. Read what the Bible says about this in Colossians 1:18-19.

What are your favorite Bible stories involving Jesus?

_____

_____

_____

The parts of the Gospels about Jesus that appeal to you the most might be an indication of your own spiritual gift(s)!
- Do you love the story of Jesus calling Zacchaeus out of the tree and going to his house for dinner? Maybe you have the gift of hospitality.
- Do the many accounts of Jesus healing the sick delight you? Maybe you have the gift of mercy.
- Do the stories of Jesus talking to Nicodemus by night or the woman at the well by day motivate you? Maybe Jesus' gift of evangelism is alive in you.
- Do you love the powerful beauty of the Sermon on the Mount? Perhaps the gift of teaching has been entrusted to you.
- Do you admire the way Jesus organized and motivated 12 men to launch a movement that has spread throughout the earth? It could be that God has given you the stewardship of the gift of administration or leadership.
- Or do you really like best the time Jesus cleared the temple court? Maybe you have the gift of prophecy.

While on earth Jesus had full possession of all the spiritual gifts. When He ascended to the Father and sent the Holy Spirit as He had promised, Jesus distributed His gifts throughout His new body, the church. Learn more about this by reading Ephesians 4:7-8,11-12.

Jesus is the only person who ever lived who possessed every spiritual gift. No individual believer will ever duplicate that. Not you. Not your pastor. Nobody. Have you ever heard, "You're the only Jesus some people will ever see"? That makes a good bumper

He is also the head of the body, the church; He is the beginning, the firstborn from the dead, so that He might come to have first place in everything. Because all the fullness was pleased to dwell in Him (Col. 1:18-19).

Grace was given to each one of us according to the measure of the Messiah's gift. For it says: When He ascended on high, He took prisoners into captivity; He gave gifts to people. And He personally gave some to be apostles, some prophets, some evangelists, some pastors and teachers, for the training of the saints in the work of ministry, to build up the body of Christ (Eph. 4:7-8,11-12).

sticker, but it is weak theology. Change it to this: "Your church is the only Jesus some people will ever see" and you're more on target!

God wants your community to see a clear, complete, and compelling picture of everything Jesus is and does. They can only experience the fullness of Jesus in the context of a local church where all members are exercising the gifts bestowed on them by the risen Christ. That's why it is so important that you do your part by discovering and using your spiritual gift. Jesus drew people to Himself. A church that reflects the breadth of His life and work will be a magnetic fellowship drawing people to Jesus. It can truly be the body of Christ in its community.

Underline or circle the words *each* and *every* in Ephesians 4:16 and 1 Peter 4:10-11.

It takes each one doing his or her part in the power of the Holy Spirit to present the world a complete picture of the person and work of Jesus the Messiah. Have you ever been moved by the power of a choir and orchestra performing the majestic "Hallelujah Chorus" from Handel's *Messiah*? How would you feel if someone asked you to perform it solo? Of course, that would be ridiculous! It would be impossible for any one person to sing and play all the parts of *Messiah*, the great musical masterpiece. Think how much more impossible it would be for any one person to try to represent the fullness of Messiah Jesus, the Master of the universe.

Jesus fully possessed and exercised every spiritual gift, including the "supplemental gifts" of miracles, healings, wisdom, knowledge, faith, and discernment. Though there is no record of Jesus speaking in or interpreting tongues, since He created languages, that would be a safe assumption. If celibacy and martyr are indeed spiritual gifts, Jesus is the supreme model for those as well.

In our study we will focus our attention mainly on the 17 gifts in the table below.

From Him the whole body, fitted and knit together by every supporting ligament, promotes the growth of the body for building up itself in love by the proper working of each individual part (Eph. 4:16).

Based on the gift they have received, everyone should use it to serve others, as good managers of the varied grace of God. If anyone speaks, his speech should be like the oracles of God; if anyone serves, his service should be from the strength God provides, so that in everything God may be glorified through Jesus Christ. To Him belong the glory and the power forever and ever (1 Pet. 4:10-11).

Support	Sharing	Speaking	Supplemental
Service/Helps	Hospitality	Shepherding	Wisdom
Giving	Mercy	Exhortation	Discernment
Administration	Apostleship	Teaching	Knowledge
Leadership	Evangelism	Prophecy	Faith

Below you will find a brief job description of these gifts. Fill in the blank in front of each description with the name of the gift you think it describes. Check off each gift in the table on the previous page as you complete the blanks.

1. _____. Lead the body by steering others to remain on task. Enable the body to organize according to God-given purposes and long-term goals.

2. _____. Motivate the body to look beyond its walls in order to carry out the Great Commission. Plant churches and serve as missionaries.

3. _____. Aid the body by recognizing the true intentions of those within or related to the body. Test the message and actions of others for the protection and well-being of the body.

4. _____. Lead others to Christ effectively and enthusiastically. Build up the body by adding new members to its fellowship.

5. _____. Encourage members to be involved in and enthusiastic about the work of the Lord; often good counselors. Motivate others to serve.

6. _____. Trust God to work beyond the human capabilities of the people. Encourage others to trust in God in the face of apparently insurmountable odds.

7. _____. Financially support with joy and generosity the work and mission of the body.

8. _____. Make visitors, guests, and strangers feel at ease. Often use their home to entertain guests. Integrate new members into the body.

9. _____. The God-given ability to learn, know, and communicate the precious truths of God's Word.

10. _____. Direct members to accomplish the goals and objectives of the church. See and communicate a vision about the future of the church. Motivate people to work together in unity to fulfill the church's mission and purposes.

11. _____. Characterized by cheerful acts of compassion. Empathize with hurting people. Keep the body healthy and unified by keeping others aware of the needs within the church.

12. _____. Proclaim the Word of God boldly to build up the body and lead to conviction of sin.

13. _____. Recognize practical needs in the body and joyfully give assistance to meet those needs. Do not mind working behind the scenes.

Service/Helps

Hospitality

Shepherding

Wisdom

Giving

Mercy

Exhortation

Discernment

Administration

Apostleship

Teaching

Knowledge

Leadership

Evangelism

Prophecy

Faith

14. _____. Look out for the spiritual welfare and development of a group of believers.

15. _____. Instruct members in the truths and doctrines of God's Word for the purposes of building up, unifying, and maturing the body.

16. _____. Discern the work of the Holy Spirit in the body and apply His teachings and actions to the needs of the body.[1]

Your answers should be in alphabetical order! The Greek alphabet starts with *alpha* and ends with *omega*. In Revelation Jesus is called the Alpha and Omega. He is the only person who has ever lived who could ever accomplish everything on the list above. The composite job description above would be overwhelming for any individual believer, wouldn't it? But it is a pretty good job description for a church. Think what a complete picture of Jesus your community would see if each of these gifts was being exercised through your church.

Go back and place a checkmark or star by one or two of the gifts that might describe you. As you look at each gift, praise Jesus for being administrator, apostle, evangelist, and so on throughout the list. Make this a regular part of your prayer time during the weeks of this study.

1. Definitions adapted from C. Gene Wilkes, *Jesus on Leadership: Becoming a Servant Leader* (Nashville: LifeWay Press, 1996), 57–58.

DAY 4
Spiritual Gifts Defined

Are you ready for a definition? *A spiritual gift is a God-given assignment, capacity, and desire to perform a function within the body of Christ with supernatural joy, energy, and effectiveness.*

Let's take a closer look at each part of that definition.

A spiritual gift is a God-given assignment, capacity and desire.

According to 1 Corinthians 12:11,18, who decides how to gift you?

God chooses your gift(s). He alone decides. He doesn't give you a gift certificate so that you can pick the ones you want. You don't get to choose your gift. You can only choose to unwrap your gift and use it. The good news is that you don't have to earn your gift either!

Charisma (plural *charismata*, from which we get *charismatic*) is the main Greek word translated *spiritual gift* or *gift* in the New Testament. Its root word is *charis*, which means *grace*. That's why some people prefer to call them grace gifts. You don't even have to ask God for your gift! Of course, you should pray that He will reveal your gift to you. The day you put your trust in Jesus Christ, the Holy Spirit took up residence within you along with the gift(s) God had predetermined for you. This spiritual birthday present is indicative of what God wants to accomplish through your new life. It's your assignment.

I learned a lot about assignments while serving in the United States Air Force. Motivated to join only by the draft notice that had interrupted my premed studies, I was not a happy camper. As the end of basic training grew near, so did my anxiety. I had taken test after test to determine my aptitude. I had filled out forms to indicate my preferences for job type and geographical location. If I could get a job assignment in the medical field and a duty assignment in a hospital in my native Texas, I reasoned, then maybe I could make more sense of what was happening in my life.

I opened the envelope. My basic-training graduation present, if you please! My assignment: communications specialist, McChord

---

A spiritual gift is a God-given assignment, capacity, and desire to perform a function within the body of Christ with supernatural joy, energy, and effectiveness.

One and the same Spirit is active in all these, distributing to each one as He wills. But now God has placed the parts, each one of them, in the body just as He wanted (1 Cor. 12:11,18).

Air Force Base, Tacoma, Washington. That is not what I wanted. But it was my assignment. I now understand that God was in the assignment too. Two important spiritual markers in my life happened in Washington state: my baptism and my call to vocational ministry. God's assignment is always right.

With your assignment God gives you the capacity to develop your gift. Some people define spiritual gifts as *God-given ability*. I prefer the word *capacity* because it suggests room for growth and improvement. I received 12 weeks of intensive communications training before reporting to my Tacoma assignment. Lots of on-the-job training followed. Learning and training were continuous. So it is with spiritual gifts.

Along with your gift will also come a divinely inspired desire. As you begin to exercise your spiritual gift, your motivation will become more and more "want to" rather than "ought to" or "have to!"

If you had no restrictions (money, time, health, family issues, etc.), what would you like to accomplish for God?

_____

_____

What spiritual gift(s) might be helpful? _____

_____

It could be that what you think about when you are doing some "spiritual daydreaming" might be indicative of the inner desire resulting from your spiritual gift(s).

To perform a function within the body of Christ
Ephesians 4:12 declares that God gave gifts "for the training of the saints in the work of ministry." Spiritual gifts are equipment, not jewelry; tools, not toys or trophies. They are standard equipment, not accessories. In Ephesians 4:12 "training" means *to prepare*. But the same Greek word can also describe an action done to repair. It is the word used to describe the mending and preparation of a fisherman's nets (Matt. 4:21) and the restoration of a relationship gone bad (Gal. 6:1).

Which gifts might primarily function to prepare people or things?

_____

_____

_____

... for the training of the saints in the work of ministry, to build up the body of Christ (Eph. 4:12).

Going on from there, He saw two other brothers, James the son of Zebedee, and his brother John. They were in a boat with Zebedee their father, mending their nets, and He called them (Matt. 4:21).

Brothers, if someone is caught in any wrongdoing, you who are spiritual should restore such a person with a gentle spirit, watching out for yourselves so you won't be tempted also (Gal. 6:1).

Which gifts might primarily function to repair people or things?

_____

_____

Ephesians 4:12 continues, "to build up the body of Christ."
Spiritual gifts should benefit the body of Christ. They should never
be used in such a way as to bring discredit on the church. That
is why the exercise of spiritual gifts is subject to the supervision
and approval of the church and its leaders. Paul reminded Timothy
that he and the elders had officially recognized Timothy's gift and
commissioned him to use it as their representative. They confirmed
the gifts they saw at work in Timothy's life and commissioned
him to use them (1 Tim. 4:14; 2 Tim. 1:6).

Have you ever observed or participated in "laying hands" on
someone as they were ordained to the ministry or commissioned
before leaving for a mission trip? My own experiences of this
nature have been key markers in my spiritual journey. The first
time will always be the most significant: when I was ordained
to the deacon ministry by the Azorean Baptist Church on the
tiny Portuguese island of Terceira.

Just like Timothy, I sometimes need to be reminded of the call
and commitment to servant leadership that event represented (see
1 Pet. 4:10). You need not be ordained to begin to use your gift,
but you should seek affirmation and confirmation from those in
the body of Christ who have observed your life and service.

Maybe we should do more informal laying on of hands. Imagine
what excitement would break forth in our churches if more people
placed their hands on another's shoulder and said, "I believe God
blesses me through you because He has given you the gift of
_____."

At the close of his extensive teaching on spiritual gifts in
1 Corinthians 12 and just before the poetic love chapter of
chapter 13, Paul wrote, "But desire the greater gifts" (1 Cor. 12:31).

The verb Paul used is plural. This is not a command to
individuals to seek certain gifts for themselves but to the church
collectively to desire all that is best for the body of Christ. God
wants us to identify spiritual gifts in others, especially those gifts
with great impact in His kingdom.

Do you recognize a spiritual gift in another person? Who? What gift?

_____

_____

*Do not neglect the gift that
is in you; it was given to
you through prophecy,
with the laying on of hands
by the council of elders
(1 Tim. 4:14).*

*I remind you to keep ablaze
the gift of God that is in you
through the laying on of my
hands (2 Tim. 1:6).*

*Based on the gift they have
received, everyone should
use it to serve others, as
good managers of the varied
grace of God (1 Pet. 4:10).*

There are different gifts, but the same Spirit. There are different ministries, but the same Lord. And there are different activities, but the same God is active in everyone and everything (1 Cor. 12:4-6).

With supernatural joy, energy, and effectiveness

At the root of the word *charis* (grace) is *char*, which means *joy*. When you discover your spiritual gift and put it to work in a ministry, you should experience a deep sense of joy. You could call spiritual gifts joy gifts as well as grace gifts. In 1 Corinthians 12:4-6 Paul implies that the whole Trinity is involved when spiritual gifts are exercised:

The word translated *activities* could also be translated *effects* or *results*. You can see the English word *energy* in the Greek word *energemata*. When you exercise your spiritual gift, God provides the energy and takes care of the results. Spiritual gifts are not intended by God for you to do busy work. They are intended to produce meaningful, purposeful results.

What kind of volunteer work gives you the most joy?

_____

_____

Your answer could provide another clue about your spiritual gift(s).

Most Christians long to experience a sense of call, a capacity to contribute, and an inner feeling of joy, power, and purpose. That's what is in store for those who will discover their spiritual gift and use it!

Ask God to bring to mind someone who has ministered to you. Pray for an appropriate time to affirm them and the impact of their gifts on your life.

DAY 5
Rewards and Roadblocks

Discovering your spiritual gift(s) offers many rewards. Along the way you'll find some roadblocks too. Let's consider the rewards first.

Rewards

When Paul wrote to the church at Rome about spiritual gifts, he was a lot more positive than in his letter to the Corinthians. Read Romans 12:1-2.

These familiar verses, often quoted to call Christians to lives of holiness and service, are actually Paul's way of introducing the church in Rome to the doctrine of spiritual gifts. Discovering your spiritual gift will help you know and test God's will for your Christian life. But that's not all. Paul continues. Read Romans 12:3.

The process of gift discovery helps you esteem yourself and others more accurately. Understanding spiritual gifts will help you understand why other believers—and even other churches and other denominations—see situations in a way that is different from the way you see it. You will be slower to criticize other Christians. In fact, I hope you develop a wonderful new habit of trying to catch somebody doing something right.

In your Bible read 1 Corinthians 12:12-27. Paul employs a wonderful analogy. The passage leads you to imagine the parts of the human body in conversation.

Read that passage, then try your hand at paraphrasing it using a different analogy from your own experiences (an athletic team; a band or an orchestra; a school, a factory, or a company; a car engine; a toolbox; a computer system, etc.).

_____
_____
_____
_____
_____
_____
_____

Brothers, by the mercies of God, I urge you to present your bodies as a living sacrifice, holy and pleasing to God; this is your spiritual worship. Do not be conformed to this age, but be transformed by the renewing of your mind, so that you may discern what is the good, pleasing, and perfect will of God (Rom. 12:1-2).

By the grace given to me, I tell everyone among you not to think of himself more highly than he should think. Instead, think sensibly, as God has distributed a measure of faith to each one (Rom. 12:3).

23

When you discover your perfect place in the body of Christ, you will have a God-ordained priority system for being a good steward of the time you spend in God's service. You may have to change from trying to do everything to doing something, from dabbling to doing one or two things well.

When you know your gift, and your motive is having ample time and energy to use it, you will learn how to say a holy no sometimes. You will be better equipped to handle the false guilt associated with saying no to some opportunities that would be better accomplished by those with other gifts.

As a steward of your gifts, you will budget your time and energy so that you can say yes when opportunities arise that match your gift. As you employ good gift management, you will be more likely to experience God's power and enthusiasm in your work for Him. You will avoid spiritual burnout. You will increasingly discover that the greatest reward of discovering and using your spiritual gift is the reassurance of God's presence and power in your life. You will have a growing awareness that God is ministering to others through you. As God unleashes His power through your spiritual gifts, you will really understand what it means to be a blessing to others.

Roadblocks

Are you fired up about stirring up your gift? Before you do, make note of some roadblocks to avoid in the process of discovering and exercising your spiritual gift.

Edify—the root word of *edifice*, a building, meaning *to build up*

1. Improper motives. The proper motive for using your gift is to bring honor to God by edifying others, letting God love people through you. Self-edification—building up yourself—should never be your primary motive. The Holy Spirit, the agent of spiritual gifts, never draws attention to Himself but always to God the Father through the Lord Jesus Christ.

You do not have because you do not ask. You ask and don't receive because you ask wrongly, so that you may spend it on your desires for pleasure (Jas. 4:2-3).

Read James 4:2d-3, then pause for a moment and pray. Ask God to help you discover your spiritual gift. Promise to put it to work in a ministry to help others and point others to Him.

2. Failure to distinguish spiritual gifts from natural gifts. Natural gifts or talents are the products of genetics, environment, or education. A capacity for knowledge, skill in speech, athletic prowess, musical ability, or a pleasing personality can be inherited or learned. God has blessed both lost and saved persons with such natural gifts. These natural gifts usually edify the individual and bring him or her honor.

Spiritual gifts are the products of the Holy Spirit's residence in a person's life. Only people who have experienced the gift of salvation have received the "birthday present" of a spiritual gift. When used properly, these gifts edify others and bring honor to God.

Ultimately, God is the source of both kinds of gifts (see Jas. 1:16-18 and Ps. 139:13-14). He weaves them beautifully together, along with the other aspects of our personality, when we yield all these components of our lives to Him in "living sacrifice" (Rom. 12:1). Sometimes God uses a natural gift as a vehicle for a spiritual gift, but He is not bound to do so.

3. Using your spiritual gift as a loophole for avoiding universal Christian responsibilities. Almost every spiritual gift listed in the New Testament represents a supernatural capacity to execute a universal responsibility expected of all Christians. All Christians are commanded to give, serve, witness, lead and teach their household, show mercy and hospitality, seek wisdom, grow in knowledge and faith, and practice spiritual discernment. In fact, gifts are usually discovered by trying many roles and determining which ones(s) God blesses with edifying results.

What's the difference? Your gift determines the kinds of needs you go out of your way to meet, tasks you go out of your way to do, persons to whom you go out of your way to share God's love. Every Christian is responsible for fulfilling universal responsibilities along the way. As you go through your daily life, sometimes you are the only one available to "love your neighbor as yourself," even if it's not your gift! So, like the good Samaritan, you respond to the best of your ability to meet the immediate need. Then you can enlist the help of others who are better gifted to meet the needs long-term. We will examine this principle more closely in week 6.

4. Lack of love. Probably the most significant roadblock can be expressed mathematically:

A gift of the Spirit − the fruit of the Spirit = 0

That is the message of 1 Corinthians 13. Paul's placement of the love passage in the middle of his teaching on spiritual gifts is not coincidental! The fruit of the Spirit reflect God's character—what a disciple is. The gifts of the Spirit reflect God's work—what a disciple does. This principle is so important, we will revisit it on the final day of our study.

Don't be deceived, my dearly loved brothers. Every generous act and every perfect gift is from above, coming down from the Father of lights; with Him there is no variation or shadow cast by turning. By His own choice, He gave us a new birth by the message of truth so that we would be the firstfruits of His creatures (Jas. 1:16-18).

It was You who created my inward parts; You knit me together in my mother's womb. I will praise You because I am unique in remarkable ways. Your works are wonderful, and I know this very well (Ps. 139:13-14).

Brothers, by the mercies of God, I urge you to present your bodies as a living sacrifice, holy and pleasing to God; this is your spiritual worship (Rom. 12:1).

The fruit of the Spirit is love, joy, peace, patience, kindness, goodness, faith, gentleness, self-control. Against such things there is no law. (Gal. 5:22-23).

Read Galatians 5:22-23. Invite the Holy Spirit to make you that kind of person the rest of the day. Write or draw your invitation below.

_____

_____

_____

_____

_____

_____

_____

_____

_____

_____

_____

_____

_____

_____

Gifts That Get Things Done

This week you will—

- grow in your appreciation for the support gifts that guide the work of the church and get that work done;
- learn how the gift of leadership guides God's people to attempt great goals;
- learn how the gift of administration organizes God's people to accomplish those goals;
- learn the importance of the gifts of service and helps;
- learn how the gift of giving provides extra resources to accomplish kingdom goals.

Supporting the Kingdom Enterprise

The support gifts could also be called *enterprise* gifts. While trying to choose a word to describe this week's group of gifts, I asked my wife what she thought of when she heard the word *enterprise*. Her immediate response: *"Star Trek!"* Our youngest son is an avid Trekkie, so I understood her answer. I was initially disappointed, however, because I was thinking of *enterprise* as a business term. But it occurred to me that the adventures of the Starship *Enterprise* are, in fact, a great analogy to describe these gifts.

We are intrigued and inspired by those who "boldly go where no one has gone before." Captains Kirk, Picard, Sisko, and Janeway keep the *Star Trek* crews focused on their mission. Regarded highly by the officers and crew, they make strategic and timely decisions, cultivate harmony, and inspire teamwork. On the *Enterprise* "Aye, Sir" is said with respect and perhaps even love (except for Mr. Spock). Those in the body of Christ who command that kind of respect and response have the gift of leadership.

In *Star Trek* the officers on the bridge organize and communicate the mission to the crew. God has gifted those who "steer" the church with administration. Then there are hundreds of crew members who go about their assigned duties with few "lines." In the army of the Lord, God has assigned many people the gifts of service and helps. All the recognition they long for is to hear the Captain of their salvation (Heb. 2:10, KJV) say, "Well done!"

Funding the Starship *Enterprise* must be an enormous challenge. So is funding the kingdom enterprise. Those with the gift of giving help underwrite the cost of expanding the kingdom of God.

This Week's Key Verse

From Him the whole body, fitted and knit together by every supporting ligament, promotes the growth of the body for building up itself in love by the proper working of each individual part (Eph. 4:16).

This Week's Lessons

Day 1: The Support Gifts

Day 2: The Gift of Leadership

Day 3: The Gift of Administration

Day 4: The Gifts of Service and Helps

Day 5: The Gift of Giving

It became him, for whom are all things, and by whom are all things, in bringing many sons unto glory, to make the captain of their salvation perfect through sufferings (Heb. 2:10, KJV).

DAY 1

The Support Gifts

Construction fascinates me. Have you ever stood at the foot of a tall skyscraper and marveled about how the architect ever envisioned it? Or pondered how much coordination it took to get it off the ground or keep it from tumbling down?

How about highway construction? Week after week you creep past the big machines, wondering, *Will they ever get finished?* Then one day the barricades are gone, and you're cruising smoothly along. And after just a few more days, you're already taking the new road for granted. Yet somebody "saw" that highway a long time before construction ever began. Somebody else understood the vision and translated it into concrete and bridges and signs. In offices far away from the construction site, someone ordered materials and filed forms. Of course, the highway never would have been completed save for the workers, those men and women who actually delivered the materials and did the physical labor!

To get the job done everybody had to do his or her assigned part. That's how the church is supposed to work too. The support gifts help the church get things done!

Review the key verse from week 1, 1 Peter 4:10, and fill in the blanks.

"Based on the gift they have received, everyone should use it to _____ others, as good managers of the varied grace of God."

Based on the gift they have received, everyone should use it to serve others, as good managers of the varied grace of God (1 Pet. 4:10).

All spiritual gifts are given for the purpose of serving others. In our study we will emphasize that the only way to discover a spiritual gift is to try it! But you must first be willing to walk through the door marked Service. The word translated *service* is the same word rendered *ministry*. Christian educator Kenneth Gangel says that the gifts of service and helps "represent the cocoon in which all the other more specialized gifts are contained."[1]

Perhaps a word of caution needs to be added here. We need to be careful not to confuse a servant spirit with the gift of serving. Not everyone who has one gift in this area automatically has any other gift, yet people with gifts of serving/helps or giving are often called to leadership or administrative roles. When people see their dedication to the task, desire to serve, and love and commitment to their church, servant models are asked to take on leadership or administrator roles. Sometimes they fit, and sometimes they don't. It just depends on each person's gift mix. You may only know whether such a role fits by trying it! And if it doesn't, that's OK. Just keep on serving, using your gifts in ways that fit you.

According to the verses below, does a leader ever graduate from being a servant? _____

- Mark 10:42-43
- 1 Peter 5:1-3

A leader never graduates from service. A biblical leader is a servant leader. The gifts of leadership and administration may be discovered and confirmed through exercising the roles of servant, helper, and shepherd. But that does not automatically mean that those who are good servants, helpers, or shepherds will be effective in leadership or administrative roles.

If you discover that God has given you the gift of leadership or administration, one of the best ways to develop that gift is to help a more experienced leader or administrator. That same apprenticeship principle applies to all the other gifts as well. That does not mean you can learn a gift from a gifted person. It does mean that you can more fully develop the capacity and desire inherent in your gift if you will spend time with someone who has been effectively using that gift for a long time.

Another foundational principle in our study is that every spiritual gift has a corresponding responsibility that all Christians are expected to fulfill along the way. For most of us, the most important place along the way is our own home. For many of us, the along-the-way place where we spend the most time is the workplace. Some spend considerable amounts of along-the-way place time as students.

Gifted or not, we must be spiritual leaders in our homes. If we are parents, we have the primary responsibility for the education of our children, especially in teaching them about the ways of God. Above all, at home, school, or work, we must be willing to serve others. That does not mean that we say yes to everything. Our spiritual gifts help us determine that. Sometimes we have to say no to other opportunities for service, especially out-of-the-way

Jesus called them over and said to them, "You know that those who are regarded as rulers of the Gentiles dominate them, and their men of high positions exercise power over them. But it must not be like that among you. On the contrary, whoever wants to become great among you must be your servant" (Mark 10:42-43).

As a fellow elder and witness to the sufferings of the Messiah, and also a participant in the glory about to be revealed, I exhort the elders among you: shepherd God's flock among you, not overseeing out of compulsion but freely, according to God's will; not for the money but eagerly; not lording it over those entrusted to you, but being examples to the flock (1 Pet. 5:1-3).

opportunities. We must, however, always exhibit the attitude of a servant. (Note: We'll explore the along-the-way, out-of-the-way principle more fully in week 6.)

Somebody Ought to ...
Imagine that you are walking down the hall at church. You spot a gum wrapper on the floor. Below, circle the number before the example that most closely approximates your initial response. (Be honest!)

___ 1. You think, *Somebody needs to teach respect for God's house.*

___ 2. You feel, *That makes me so angry! I wish I knew who did that so I could straighten them out!*

___ 3. You think, *I've seen a lot of that lately. Maybe we need some more trash cans in this hallway.*

___ 4. You act: *I'll pick that up and put it in the trash.*

Now go back and put the first letter of the gift you think it might indicate: A for *administration*; P for *prophecy*; S for *service*; T for *teacher*.

The teacher (1) and the prophet (2) would most likely address the situation by speaking about it. The gifted administrator (3) sees a problem and thinks about a possible solution. The person with the gift of service (4) just does something about it. Sometimes the things that concern us might help us identify our spiritual gift.

What's been concerning you lately at church?

_____

_____

What could you do about it? What spiritual gift(s) might help?

_____

_____

Take a few moments to pray. Tell God about some things at church that are bothering you. Listen to Him speak to your heart about those issues. Be careful! He may have you in mind as a solution. If He does, you can be sure that He has gifted you to respond effectively, and in such a way that it is for the common good, building up the church, so that He is glorified.

---

1. Kenneth Gangel, *Unwrap Your Spiritual Gifts* (Wheaton: Victor, 1983), 89.

DAY 2

The Gift of Leadership

Watching an orchestra performance has taken on a new meaning for me since I discovered that the word for "common good" in 1 Corinthians 12:7 is the Greek *sympheron*. I love to listen to the warm-up, when all the musicians are tuning their instruments. Finally they stop. As if on cue, the audience grows quiet in anticipation. The conductor enters. He is greeted with applause not just from the audience but from the orchestra as well. The players recognize the leader's ability to guide them. The conductor shakes the hand of the orchestra master, seated in the first chair in the violin section. (The leader is often a leader of leaders.) Then he steps up to the stand. With all eyes focused on him, he raises the baton. One quick downward motion, and beautiful music begins.

Have you ever pretended to be an orchestra conductor? Do you mind being in front of people? Are you comfortable being the center of attention? Do you long to see a group of God's people work together to accomplish something significant for His glory? Do others tend to follow you? If you answered yes to any of these questions, God may have entrusted you with the gift of leadership. If not, you will still want to learn what motivates gifted leaders.

To each one the manifestation of the Spirit is given for the common good (1 Cor. 12:7, NIV).

Refer back to week 1, day 3, and complete the definition of the gift of leadership: Direct members to accomplish the goals and objectives of the church. See and communicate a _____ about the future of the church. _____ people to work together in _____ to fulfill the church's mission and purposes.

Leaders have *vision*. Leaders stand on undeveloped plots of land and see buildings. Leaders stand in empty classrooms and see people milling around. Leaders stand behind pulpits in empty worship centers and see people walking down the aisle to follow Christ.

Those with the gift of leadership also have followers! These followers are *motivated* by the leader to accomplish the vision. They don't simply follow blindly. They want to follow and work. Perhaps most important in distinguishing those in authority with the gift of leadership from those without it is their unusual ability to help people work *in unity* to accomplish the vision and to deal effectively with any opposition that threatens the harmony of the group.

The Greek word translated "leading" in Romans 12:8 means *to stand before, be over.* The King James Version translates the word "ruleth." That word has a bad connotation for some people, especially those of us who live in a democratic society. That's why Paul instructs those with the gift of leadership how to use the gift.

If exhorting, in exhortation; giving, with generosity; leading, with diligence; showing mercy, with cheerfulness (Rom. 12:8).

Complete the phrase about the gift of leadership from Romans 12:8: "If … leading, with _____."

The person with the gift of leadership is instructed to govern with *diligence.* The word *diligence* includes the ideas of hard work, earnestness, and zeal. Those with the gift of leadership certainly exhibit those traits. But the word also includes the idea of care and carefulness. One with the gift of leadership cares not only for the cause but also for the people involved in the cause. Jesus is the foremost example of the gift of leadership.

Moses and Misconceptions About the Gift of Leadership

Moses is the outstanding example of a leader in the Old Testament. Let's look at some of the highlights from his life and evaluate how Moses stacks up against some popular misconceptions about leadership.

Misconception 1. Real leaders take charge without being personally enlisted. They rise up voluntarily to respond to God's vision.

Read Exodus 3:10,16-17. What was the vision/mission God had in mind for Moses?

_____

_____

Read Exodus 3:11-13; 4:1. What were Moses' concerns about accepting the responsibility to implement God's vision? Do you think Christian leaders today wrestle with some of those same issues?

_____

_____

Misconception 2. A person must be a good speaker to be an effective leader.

Read Exodus 4:10-16. Do you think Moses was really a poor speaker, or was he just making an excuse? What provision did God make for taking care of this perceived handicap?

_____

_____

Misconception 3. Leaders manage time and handle details naturally.

Read Exodus 18:13-26. Summarize Jethro's father-in-law advice to Moses. What principles of leadership in this passage might help church leaders handle their shepherding role?

_____

_____

Misconception 4. The majority will always affirm the vision of a gifted leader.

Scan Numbers 13–14 to recall the crisis at Kadesh-Barnea. Can you recall a time when the majority "voted down" an opportunity to do something important for the Lord?

_____

_____

Just as in the case of Moses, the gift of leadership often has to be called out. Leadership is enhanced by effective speech, but it does not require it. Gifted leaders sometimes need help with administration. (We'll explore that relationship tomorrow.) Sometimes even the most gifted leader faces opposition. Armed with the gift of leadership, he or she can handle all of these challenges!

What gifted leaders have touched your life?

_____

_____

Take a few minutes to thank God for them.

Moses replied to the LORD, "Please, Lord, I have never been eloquent—either in the past or recently or since You have been speaking to Your servant—because I am slow and hesitant in speech" (Ex. 4:10).

"What you're doing is not good," Moses' father-in-law said to him. "You will certainly wear out both yourself and these people who are with you, because the task is too heavy for you. You can't do it alone." Moses listened to his father-in-law and did everything he said. So Moses chose able men from all Israel and made them leaders over the people as officials of thousands, hundreds, fifties, and tens. They judged the people at all times; the hard cases they would bring to Moses, but every minor case they would judge themselves (Ex. 18:17-18,24-26).

DAY 3

The Gift of Administration

The gifts of leadership and administration have a number of similarities. Some teachers even suggest that they are essentially one gift. We will treat them as two related but different gifts. Since there are two different Greek words, we are certainly safe in doing so.

The leader and the administrator are sometimes hard to tell apart. Usually, only the person with the gift can tell you which gift provides motivation. Since their ministry responsibilities in the church are often similar, the administrator generally learns some leadership skills, and the leader usually learns some administrative skills. Jesus has a full measure of both. The advance of Christianity throughout the world is ample evidence of His leadership gift. Every wonderful detail of creation testifies to His supremacy in administration. Few others have both gifts, but their assignments are often similar.

Yesterday we saw that the word translated "leadership" means *to stand before, to be over.* Paul used that word eight times. He used the word translated "managing" ("administration" in the NIV) only in 1 Corinthians 12:28. It is the Greek word *kubernesis.* In literature outside the Bible, this word meant *one who steers a ship.* Imagine a captain piloting a ship across a stormy ocean and safely into a distant harbor, and you've got the idea of what a person with the gift of administration is good at doing. In the King James Version the word is translated "governments."

In the business world *management* is usually the word used of those who administrate. However, in public service jobs such as schools, hospitals, and government positions, the word *administration* is more likely to be used. In Europe many key government positions actually carry the official title *minister,* which is what you get when you drop the *ad* from *administer.*

Kubernesis is also the word from which we derive *cybernetics,* the study of communication and control systems. The gifted administrator enhances the flow of information in the church. He or she will use charts, graphs, memos, newsletters, or whatever it takes to help the team understand what is happening, how the work is going, where it is going, and why we need to keep going.

God has placed these in the church: first apostles, second prophets, third teachers, next, miracles, then gifts of healing, helping, managing, various kinds of languages (1 Cor. 12:28).

In the church God has appointed first of all apostles, second prophets, third teachers, then workers of miracles, also those having gifts of healing, those able to help others, those with gifts of administration, and those speaking in different kinds of tongues (1 Cor. 12:28, NIV).

Below are some of the behaviors common to both the gifts of leadership and administration. Put a checkmark by those that might describe you. Also think about others you know who might fit these descriptions. Print their initials in the margin.

❑ Set challenging goals and are compelled to communicate them.

❑ Are enthusiastic, highly motivated, intense, and competitive.

❑ Can take the heat, enduring criticism rather than compromising high goals or standards.

❑ See potential in others and try to involve lots of people. Sometimes misunderstood and accused of using people. Both delegate as much as possible but know when they cannot.

❑ Get discouraged when goals are not achieved or progress is slower than they had hoped.

❑ Do not tolerate mistakes well or admit them easily.

Certain other characteristics distinguish the gifts of leadership and administration. Consider these three areas:

	Leadership	Administration
Vision	Receive and communicate a vision for what God desires a certain unit of the body of Christ to accomplish.	Are among the first to understand and appreciate the vision.
	See the big picture. Hate the details!	Comprehend the big picture. Clarify and communicate the vision, and marshal the resources to accomplish it. Detail oriented.
	Like an architect.	Like a contractor.
Decisions	Often make decisions based on intuition.	Usually make decisions like *Dragnet*'s Sergeant Friday: "Just the facts!"
Relationships	More comfortable in a formal setting than one on one. (So are prophets and teachers.)	Enjoy one-to-one or small-group relationships, but are best in working, task-oriented relationships. (So are exhorters and shepherds.)

In the Old Testament two of the best examples of the gift of administration are Joseph and Nehemiah. Both are great examples for those who serve in number-two positions to a leader.

We have already identified Moses as an example of a gifted leader. Two of the best examples of the gift of administration in the Old Testament are Joseph and Nehemiah. Both are great examples for those who serve in number-two positions to a leader.

When the exiles returned from Babylon to rebuild Jerusalem, they were led by a leader-administrator team: Ezra and Nehemiah.

Read Nehemiah 8. (It's just 18 verses!) What was the guidebook by which Ezra and Nehemiah directed the work of rebuilding?

_____

Ezra and Nehemiah directed the people to the Scriptures. The Bible must be the basis for leadership and administration.

Visionary goals always cause some level of opposition. You can read in both Ezra and Nehemiah about opposition to the rebuilding of the temple and the city walls. However, a person who seldom invites the counsel of others and usually ignores advice or valid complaints probably does not possess either of these gifts.

Unfortunately, certain negative behaviors are sometimes incorrectly linked to the gifts of leadership and administration. Some people are greedy for power, and such people have done much to harm churches. The gift of leadership is not granted on the basis of church office or position. Gifted leaders are always servant leaders.

Some people are skilled manipulators. They consider people just another resource to accomplish their goals. The gifted administrator or leader delegates responsibility to help develop the potential of the person enlisted, not just to achieve the goal. Building big people is as important to them as completing big projects.

A degree or job in secular management is not a valid indicator, by itself, of the spiritual gift of leadership or administration. The same principle also applies to professional educators and the gift of teaching. Of course, such training is not necessarily incompatible with these gifts, either. Too often, however, nominating committees enlist persons for committees and other positions based on professional criteria rather than on the basis of spiritual gifts. In Christ's church, committees, program organizations, and ministry teams function best when their work is directed by a person God has empowered with the gift of leadership or administration.

Do you know people God may have been entrusted with the gift of administration or leadership? Write their names here.

_____

DAY 4
The Gifts of Service and Helps

Have you ever lingered in your seat at the conclusion of a movie and read the names of the grips and gaffers and the host of other behind-the-camera people it took to bring the picture to the screen? Even in the church it's generally the "producers," the "directors," and those with the "speaking parts" who receive the most recognition. But in every healthy church are scores of people working behind the scenes for each star basking in the spotlight. These folks prefer being a member of the crew rather than the cast!

Do you prefer to work behind the scenes? Would you rather hear a sincere thank-you than to receive a certificate of appreciation in a worship service? Do you often catch yourself saying, "I'd rather not be in charge, but I'd be glad to help"? Would you rather be doing something about a problem than sitting around a commit-tee room talking about it? Do you enjoy seeing the results of your labor? Are you happier working on a series of short-term projects than writing strategic plans?

If you answered yes to a number of these questions, God may have entrusted you with the gift of service or the gift of helps.

Read Philippians 2:1-7. What does this passage teach about the proper attitude of a servant?

_____

The gifts of service and helps are supernatural expressions of this Christlike attitude. They are not leftover gifts. Service and helps are the cardiac system of the body of Christ. Without these gifts flowing throughout the body, the effectiveness of every other gift is diminished. You may recall that the word translated *service* is *diakonos*, the word from which we get *deacon*. The first deacons were selected to wait on tables and serve the widows in the church. By assuming these duties, they ensured the apostles had ample time to study and pray in preparation for preaching and teaching.

When servants and helpers do not use their gifts, those with speaking and leading gifts usually pitch in to help. But the body suffers from lack of nourishment when prophets, teachers, and exhorters do not have time to prepare. The body also suffers a lack of purpose and direction when leaders and administrators do not

If then there is any encouragement in Christ, if any consolation of love, if any fellowship with the Spirit, if any affection and mercy, fulfill my joy by thinking the same way, having the same love, sharing the same feelings, focusing on one goal. Do nothing out of rivalry or conceit, but in humil-ity consider others as more important than yourselves. Everyone should look out not only for his own interests, but also for the interests of others. Make your own attitude that of Christ Jesus, who, existing in the form of God, did not consider equality with God as something to be used for His own advantage. Instead He emptied Himself by assuming the form of a slave (Phil. 2:1-7).

37

According to the grace given to us, we have different gifts: If prophecy, use it according to the standard of faith; if service, in service (Rom. 12:6-7).

The following behaviors are common to the gifts of service and helps. Put a checkmark beside those that might describe you.
Also think about others you know who might fit these descriptions.
Print their initials in the margin.

❑ Exercise gifts primarily within the body of Christ.
❑ Display a high degree of loyalty and devotion.
❑ Like to be liked—and are usually likable!
❑ Do not need to be in the public eye to be fulfilled.
❑ Prefer to complete a task as quickly as possible. Are sometimes tempted to sacrifice quality in favor of speed!
❑ Need to know their efforts are appreciated but usually prefer personal recognition over a formal, public display.

The following chart shows some characteristics that distinguish the gifts of service and helps.

	Service	Helps
Instructions	Tend to jump right in and take care of it.	More likely to wait for instructions, the more specific the better.
Resources	Given a project to accomplish, are likely to make decisions or take initiative to secure resources to complete the task.	Tends to wait for someone else to provide the resources, or to ask for advice about what resoures to use.
Motivation	To complete the project.	To please the person helped.
Relationships	Short-term. Like to work on a variety of projects with a variety of people. In fact, don't mind working alone. Do not like the person who made the assignment to look over their shoulder.	Long-term. The relationship with the person being helped is of primary importance. Desire the person being helped to be pleased with the project. Like frequent feedback from the person helped.

Although the gifts differ, the tasks associated with them are often much the same. In fact, it is not uncommon for the person with the gift of service to have a faithful helper. In that kind of relationship, the motivation of the servant is to get the job done. The motivation of the helper is to please her coworker, the servant. The word translated "helps" or "helping," which occurs only in 1 Corinthians 12:28, includes the ideas of supporting and assisting. This is illustrated in an interesting Old Testament passage about the craftsmen selected to construct the tabernacle.

Read Exodus 31:1-6. Circle the name of the craftsman with the gift of service. Draw a box around the name of his helper.

Oholiab was gifted by God as a helper to Bezalel, the craftsman, with the gift of service. God had gifted him to beautify the tabernacle. Dozens of other servants and helpers worked under their direction. If you were playing a game of Bible trivia, and the question was "Who built the tabernacle?" you would probably answer Moses. Since he was the leader, you would be correct. But despite the vision communicated by Moses, if it had not been for the gifted servants and helpers who actually constructed it, there would have been no tabernacle.

Do you know someone who may have the gift of service?

_____

The gift of helps?

_____

Church pews are full of people with a buried gift of service or helps. God has important work for them to do! We must call them forth—for their own good and the common good of the body.

Next week we will look at four gifts whose primary passion is reaching out to those outside the body of Christ. They also need partners with gifts of serving and helps to maximize their gifts.

God has placed these in the church: first apostles, second prophets, third teachers, next, miracles, then gifts of healing, helping, managing, various kinds of languages (1 Cor. 12:28).

The LORD also spoke to Moses: "Look, I have appointed by name Bezalel son of Uri, son of Hur, of the tribe of Judah. I have filled him with God's Spirit, with wisdom, understanding, and ability in every craft to design artistic works in gold, silver, and bronze, to cut gemstones for mounting, and to carve wood for work in every craft. I have also selected Oholiab son of Ahisamach, of the tribe of Dan, to be with him" (Ex. 31:1-6).

DAY 5

The Gift of Giving

Do you have a deep desire to see God's work advance? Do you have an eye for excellence? Do you daydream about what churches, missions, and Christian organizations could accomplish if they had enough money? Do you feel a burden when persons involved on the front lines of God's kingdom work share their financial needs? Has God blessed you with an ability to make money or to be content with a simple lifestyle? If your answer to any of these questions is yes, then God may have given you the gift of giving.

Read 2 Corinthians 8:9. Did Jesus have the gift of giving?

_____

You know the grace of our Lord Jesus Christ: although He was rich, for your sake He became poor, so that by His poverty you might become rich (2 Cor. 8:9).

Jesus possessed every spiritual gift, including the gift of giving. Christ was the Lord of creation and Master of the universe long before His pilgrimage to earth. He is the supreme model of giving from a position of wealth. His earthly life as Jesus of Nazareth is the supreme example of giving from a position of material poverty. He sacrificed the splendor of heaven to live among us as one of us. Then He sacrificed His human body so that we might share that splendor with Him. Yes, Jesus has the gift of giving!

Following are some characteristics and behaviors associated with people who have the gift of giving. Put a checkmark beside those that might describe you. Also think about others you know who might fit these descriptions. Print their initials in the margin.

❏ Go beyond the Christian responsibility of giving a tithe. Give generously, with liberality, simplicity, and singleness of mind.
❏ Have pure motives. If they have an ability to make money, their motive is to earn more so they can give more. They often do not like their gifts to be widely publicized.
❏ Want their gift to be of high quality and used in a worthwhile manner. More likely to give to ministries or projects than to individuals. Not usually a soft touch but wait for projects and needs that really make a difference. Alert to needs that others overlook. "Too good," "too expensive," and "good enough for the church" are not in their vocabulary.
❏ Have a heart for missions. Sometimes misinterpret the desire to give

to missions as a call to the mission field. If a person supports 10 missionaries, he should be sure God is calling him before he stops supporting them so he can go himself.

❑ Want their gift to be administered well but do not designate every nickel. Usually do not enjoy serving on the finance committee. Want assurance that those who do serve on committees that disperse gifts are themselves obedient givers.

❑ Enjoy giving special gifts to honor those called to vocational ministry. Never attach any strings to the gift and do not want to be treated differently because of the kindness done.

God Himself was speaking through Betty the day she said, "God told me to give you my car." Even though I had prayed earnestly about our transportation needs, I argued with her! Characteristic of a giver, she said, "Don't argue with God. I'll be out tonight, but I'll leave the keys and the title under the mat. Come get it."

Seborn and Jewel, a godly older couple, wanted to buy me a new suit in honor of my 10th anniversary at the church. While we were in the store the suit grew, at their insistence, into a new wardrobe. After we returned to their home, Seborn told me that he expected no special treatment in response to their act of kindness. That's the attitude of a person with the gift of giving.

When our three sons were young, some still unknown person funded a Florida vacation for our family. My pastor came into my office one day and handed me a check. He said an anonymous person had been led by God to provide us a vacation, and the substantial amount could be used only for that purpose. Gifted givers sometimes do not want the recipient to know the source of the gift, but they want to ensure it is used for the purpose they intend. They get extra pleasure in letting the transaction be between them, God, and the messenger. Any number of people in our church could have provided that much-needed vacation.

According to the grace given to us, we have different gifts: If prophecy, use it according to the standard of faith; if service, in service; if teaching, in teaching; if exhorting, in exhortation; giving, with generosity (Rom. 12:6-8).

Do you think a person who discovers that they do not have the gift of giving is excused from tithing?   ❑ Yes ❑ No

No, the tithe is a minimum Christian responsibility. God expects 10 percent of our income to be returned to Him through our church to acknowledge that He is the owner of everything. Many people with the gift of giving would testify that a decision to become obedient to the biblical principle of the tithe was the starting point for the discovery of their gift.

41

God gives us spiritual gifts to increase our joy, not to make us miserable.

Ken testifies to the struggles he had in becoming obedient to the tithe. He discovered the gift of giving in the wake of the joy he experienced from that step of obedience. God gives us spiritual gifts to increase our joy, not to make us miserable. You can be assured that if God has given you the gift of giving, He has also given you the ability either (1) to make money or (2) to enjoy a simple lifestyle (or maybe both). The Giver always gives the giver both the gift of giving and the gift to give!

Brainstorm! What if all the members of your church with the gift of giving discovered the joy of using their gift, and the rest of the members discovered the joy of becoming obedient givers? If your church could double its budget, what would you like to see your church do with the extra funds? Make a list in the margin.

Evaluate your list. Is there a common denominator? If so, it may indicate your spiritual gift!

A believer with the gift of administration or leadership, for example, might want to remodel the building or construct a new one. One with the gift of helps might want new office equipment for the staff. Someone with the gift of service might know that the church needs to update its landscaping or kitchen equipment. One with the gift of evangelism might list witness training or missions. Someone with the gift of mercy might place a higher priority on benevolence ministries. You get the idea!

Sometimes church folks get frustrated with one another over such issues. A person with the gift of mercy may not understand why we want a new copier when so many in the community are going hungry. You can think of other examples.

What's the point? If every member of the church was obedient to tithe and several with the gift of giving supplied extra resources, there would be no need for such disagreements. We could do it all: buildings and staff salaries that honored God; food, clothing, and shelter for those in need; abundant support of missions and ministries. If all those with gifts of service and helps used their gifts, there would be plenty of enthusiastic folks to staff every ministry as well as exciting new ministries. Your community would then see a complete picture of who Jesus is and the impact He can have in the life of individuals and cultures.

Thank God for all He's given you, including the gift of salvation. Listen to Him speak to your heart about your own level of giving.

Gifts That Engage Persons Outside the Church

This week you will—
- grow in your appreciation for the sharing gifts that communicate God's love with outsiders;
- understand how the gift of hospitality makes people feel welcome;
- understand how the gift of mercy demonstrates God's love;
- understand how the gift of evangelism shares the good news;
- understand the modern-day equivalent of the gift of apostleship.

Gifts on the Edge

These gifts connect the church with those on the outskirts of the kingdom of God. They engage outsiders and welcome them into the body of Christ. The gifts we will study this week focus largely on those not yet in the body of Christ or who are at risk to slip out of active involvement. Each of these gifts engages those on the outside, helping them discover the joy of being in Christ and in a local church.

Red blood cells carry oxygen and nutrients to the other cells in the human body, constantly sustaining its many functions. White blood cells have a more specific task: targeting strangers in the body and helping alleviate or prevent dysfunction and disease. The support and speaking gifts are like red blood cells in the body of Christ. The sharing gifts are like white blood cells. They are burdened to engage the lost, the lonely, and the hurting and to introduce them to a loving, caring, forgiving God. Churches without the gifts of hospitality, mercy, and evangelism can be busy, well organized, well maintained, and biblically orthodox. But they will almost certainly be cold and uncaring.

The church is supposed to be a hospital for sinners, not a museum for saints. The sharing gifts have an outward focus, filled with the passion of Jesus "to seek and to save the lost" (Luke 19:10).

This Week's Key Verse
God has placed the parts, each one of them, in the body just as He wanted (1 Cor. 12:18).

This Week's Lessons
Day 1: The Sharing Gifts
Day 2: The Gift of Hospitality
Day 3: The Gift of Mercy
Day 4: The Gift of Evangelism
Day 5: The Gift of Apostleship

The speaking gifts we will study next week are central to the health of the church, grounding believers in the Word of God. The support gifts we studied last week keep the body of Christ organized and functioning. Those gifts function primarily within the church and among believers.

DAY 1

The Sharing Gifts

My first official position in a local church was as a Kindergarten Sunday School teacher at the First Baptist Church of Lakewood in Tacoma, Washington. One of the methods for teaching preschoolers is to use Bible thoughts in natural conversation while the children engage in various activities like creative art, nature/science, dramatic play, books, music, puzzles/manipulatives, and blocks/construction. Preschool boys plus blocks ensured that one of my most-used Bible thoughts was "Be ready to share" (based on Eph. 4:27).

Some of us learn the lesson of sharing in kindergarten, but most of us struggle our whole lives with knowing how and when to share. Why is sharing so hard? Sharing my money. Sharing my food. Sharing my clothes. Sharing my home. Sharing my car. Sharing my pew. Sharing my faith.

Go back and read the last paragraph again. Circle the word you think might be the key to understanding why many people find it difficult to share. (Hint: It's repeated several times and has only two letters!)

Sharing is a stewardship word. The first principle of Christian stewardship is "God owns everything." That includes all the things listed above. It also includes my spiritual gifts. Oops! There's that word again: *my*. I have to remind myself often that God owns everything I am and everything I possess. I am just a steward, a manager, of the relationships and resources He has entrusted to me, including *my* spiritual gifts.

God taught me that lesson clearly one day while I was mowing my lawn. It was one of those scorching hot Texas summer days. My neighbor's grass was particularly high, and I was a bit aggravated by it. As I grumbled and mumbled, God said (in one of those ways that is more audible than speech), "Why don't you mow it?" I'm ashamed to confess that, after convincing myself I wasn't deluded by heatstroke, I argued with the Father. I don't remember everything I muttered, but I closed my case with something like, "Why should I mow his grass with my lawn mower?" As though it were yesterday, I can hear God responding in my spirit, "It's not

> Most of us struggle our whole lives with knowing how and when to share.

your lawn mower. It's My lawn mower." I mowed the lawn! As I did, I *gave* my stuff back to God: His car. His house. His clothes. His food. His kids. His everything.

I still struggle with the ownership issue every day. Maybe you do too. That's why I so appreciate those with one or more of the sharing gifts. Those who have fully developed these gifts share easily and naturally.

Actually, all the spiritual gifts are for sharing. A spiritual gift has no value if it is just *my* gift. Imagine someone who claims to have the gift of giving but does not give. What good is that? By the way, you may wonder why the gift of giving is not classified as a sharing gift. It could be. You should be careful about any teaching on spiritual gifts that adamantly places the gifts into strict, indisputable categories. Earlier in this book we began with a chart that listed the gifts. It is simply a tool to provide a framework for this study and one way to group spiritual gifts, but it is certainly not a divine revelation. We will look at other groupings throughout this study. The fact that none of the lists in Paul's letters is complete argues against the creation of a strict system for understanding gifts and how they operate. Paul, under the inspiration of the Holy Spirit, was primarily communicating a simple message to the early churches: "Each of you has a gift. No one of you has all the gifts. All the gifts are important, so please try to get along with one another!"

It is impossible to draw distinct lines between the spiritual gifts. We've already seen similarities between leadership and administration, serving and helps. In some ways the line is sort of fuzzy between giving and helps. In the days to come, you will notice similarities between helps and mercy, as well as exhortation. The same is true for the gifts we will explore this week.

If there is a system to the way spiritual gifts are designed to operate, it is that everyone needs to play his or her part to make the system work. It's sort of like a baseball team. The basic skills of an infielder are relatively indistinguishable to someone who watches baseball only casually. In fact, many third basemen can perform pretty well at first base, and most shortstops can field second base just fine. But each infield position is also different, and infielders are most effective when they are playing the position where they are the strongest.

I was an all-star third baseman in Little League, with a batting average in the top 10 in the league. My first year in Pony League, I was moved to second base. Although not as challenging as third

All the spiritual gifts are for sharing. A spiritual gift has no value if it is just *my* gift.

base, I performed well and batted lead off. The next year I was placed at shortstop. Although I performed adequately in the field, I was a nervous wreck. My hitting went to pot, and I moved to ninth in the batting order. The pressure was just too great. Even if no one else knew it, I felt out of position. My love for baseball waned. I showed up for the games but with less and less passion and enthusiasm. I became a miserable ball player. The joy was gone.

Has something like that ever happened to you in a church responsibility?

_____

_____

_____

_____

It is important to discover the gift that fits you most perfectly.

That's why it is important to discover the gift that fits you most perfectly. Others may not be able to tell the difference between what motivates you and someone else, but you will know. Keep that in mind as we explore the sharing gifts.

Meditate on This Week's Key Verse
"God has placed the parts, each one of them, in the body just as He wanted" (1 Cor. 12:18).

God is the manager of His kingdom team. He knows what position He wants you to play. He has gifted you to play that position well. Spend a few moments asking Him to reveal it to you and pledge to share your gift for the benefit of others.

DAY 2
The Gift of Hospitality

Are you especially sensitive to the new person in the group or class? Are you burdened to help people who are standing around by themselves at a gathering? Do you want to introduce them to others and to make them feel included? Has anyone ever told you that you always make him or her feel at home? Do you enjoy meeting new people? Are you comfortable with strangers? Do you like getting a room or house ready for a meeting or social? If your answer to these questions is yes, God may have entrusted you with the gift of hospitality.

In Romans 12:13 and elsewhere all Christians are instructed to practice hospitality. All believers are to be "given to hospitality" (as the KJV translates that verse) along the way. But God has gifted some believers with a unique capacity for making others feel welcome. They often go out of their way to practice hospitality.

Read 1 Peter 4:9 and circle the phrase that distinguishes the gift of hospitality from the universal Christian responsibility to show hospitality.

Those with the gift of hospitality practice it *without complaining*. They open their hearts and their homes to others without grumbling.

Philadelphia is called the city of brotherly love. The *phila* part is from the Greek word for *love*. The *delphia* part is from the Greek word for *brother*. So *Philadelphia* means *love of brothers*. The Greek word translated *hospitality* is *philoxenia*. It literally means *love of strangers*.

In addition to the passages already cited (Rom. 12:13 and 1 Pet. 4:9), this word is used only three more times in the New Testament. Two of the passages are qualifications for those in vocational ministry. Circle the word in each passage that relates to loving strangers.

Have you ever heard someone complain that your pastor is more interested in new people in the church than he is the longtime members. Or that he spends a lot of time visiting guests but almost never visits in the home of the flock? Good! He's passed the test of being hospitable! Some pastors have the gift of hospitality. I know

Be hospitable to one another without complaining (1 Pet. 4:9).

This saying is trustworthy: "If anyone aspires to be an overseer, he desires a noble work." An overseer, therefore, must be above reproach, the husband of one wife, self-controlled, sensible, respectable, hospitable, an able teacher (1 Tim. 3:1-2).

An overseer, as God's manager, must be blameless, not arrogant, not quick tempered, not addicted to wine, not a bully, not greedy for money, but hospitable, loving what is good, sensible, righteous, holy, self-controlled (Titus 1:7-8).

47

many others who do not. Some of them have to work really hard at it. Others are blessed with a spouse who has an incredible measure of the gift of hospitality. Almost all pastors recognize the importance of discovering those in their church who are so gifted, and putting them to work to make sure the church is a place where people feel welcome.

The other passage that uses the *love of strangers* word is Hebrews 13:1-3. You'll recognize the passage. But the word is not always translated *hospitality*.

Be not forgetful to entertain strangers: for thereby some have entertained angels unawares (Heb. 13:2, KJV).

Don't neglect to show hospitality, for by doing this some have welcomed angels as guests without knowing it (Heb. 13:2).

Circle the word in Hebrews 13:2, KJV, that you think is the substitute. Then read HCSB translation, where the word *hospitality* is used. Compare the two translations.

This letter was written to a persecuted church, made up primarily of Jewish converts living in and around Rome. It was easy for these believers to lock themselves inside their homes, fearful even to answer a knock at their door. The writer of Hebrews challenges them to be ready to *entertain* strangers. The emphasis is really on people you don't know.

Trend watchers have noted that, for many people, houses have become fortified cocoons. After a busy day of work, perhaps a long commute, and with daily media accounts of crime and violence, it is certainly tempting to lock the doors, turn on the answering machine, grab the remote control, and cocoon.

On the other hand, I believe that while many people are cleaning and decorating their homes or manicuring their lawns, they think about having some people over to share the blessing of their home. Those who act on that inner desire may discover that God has given them the gift of hospitality.

Those with the gift of hospitality go beyond the requirements of entertainment. Entertaining is usually judged by a worldly standard: Everything was just perfect—the food, the decor, the music, the program—every*thing*. Those with the gift of hospitality put people first, not things. In fact, those with the gift of hospitality don't really care if the house is immaculate or even if there is any food in the refrigerator. You are still welcome, and you know you are!

Billy and Freida have the gift of hospitality. Together they host more Sunday School socials than any other couple in their church. Billy is a natural as a greeter. He arrives early, ready to give a genuine smile and to extend a warm handshake to members and guests alike. He makes people glad they've come to church from the moment they arrive.

Members of my family have benefited from Billy and Freida's hospitality. On a recent trip to Texas, our family crashed at their home overnight. It wasn't planned, just a spur-of-the-moment decision. They made us feel so welcome. Our oldest son even lived with them between college semesters.

Freida has a demanding job and often works long hours, but that doesn't matter. She'll still volunteer to host the swim party for her daughter's class. When their teenage son, Craig, was killed in a car accident several years ago, Billy and Freida could easily have cocooned. But they didn't. They can't! God has placed inside them the gift of hospitality, and they enjoy His pleasure when they exercise it.

The world shouts, "Look at my house. Look at my car. Look at all my stuff." The gift of hospitality whispers, "Whether little or much, fancy or plain, what's mine is yours. So make yourself at home. You are welcome here."

How do you discover if God has given you the gift of hospitality? Try some of the ideas listed below. If you experience joy, energy, and effectiveness, hospitality is probably your gift! List a couple of other ideas too.

❑ Volunteer to be the hospitality leader in an Adult Sunday School department or class. Take responsibility for Sunday-morning refreshments.

❑ Serve as a member of the greeter team. Ask the pastor or staff if greeters are needed in the parking lot, at the entrances to the church building, or at the guest/information desk. Or volunteer to serve as a greeter for your Sunday School department or class, paying special attention to making newcomers feel welcome.

❑ Join the women's ministry welcome team that takes information to newcomers in your city (or start one)!

❑ Host the next Sunday School class or choir fellowship.

❑ Volunteer to be the fellowship leader in your Sunday School department or class.

❑ Organize and take a meal to a new mom and dad or a bereaved member.

❑ Take a snack pack to a family in the ICU waiting room.

The world shouts, "Look at my house. Look at my car. Look at all my stuff." The gift of hospitality whispers, "Whether little or much, fancy or plain, what's mine is yours. So make yourself at home. You are welcome here."

Some people think you should first identify your spiritual gift, then get involved in a ministry to use it. Actually, most people discover their spiritual gift in just the opposite way! They volunteer for a ministry or start a new one and discover if they are gifted for it in the course of doing it.

Some people think you should first identify your spiritual gift, then get involved in a ministry to use it. Actually, most people discover their spiritual gift in just the opposite way! They volunteer for a ministry or start a new one and discover if they are gifted for it in the course of doing it. Do you know someone whose gift might be hospitality? How could that person be enlisted to serve in a ministry like the ones above?

_____

_____

_____

_____

What ministries have you tried to see if you have the gift of hospitality? Reflect on those experiences.

_____

_____

_____

_____

What ministries can you try to explore this gift?

_____

_____

_____

DAY 3
The Gift of Mercy

How do you feel when you are around people who are dirty, sick, outcast, poor, aged, mentally ill, physically handicapped, deformed, hungry, shut-in, retarded, educationally deprived, underclothed, depressed, bereaved, lonely, derelict, alcoholic, abused, addicted, imprisoned, illiterate, orphaned, or widowed? If you have a strong desire to relieve the suffering of one or more of these types of persons, God may have entrusted you with the gift of mercy.

Read Romans 12:6-8 and circle the phrase that distinguishes the gift of mercy from the universal Christian responsibility to be merciful.

Those with the gift of mercy exercise it cheerfully. The Greek word for *cheerful* is *hilarotes,* from which we get the English words *hilarity* and *hilarious.* In his classic commentary Matthew Henry amplifies the definition aptly as "pleasant looks and gentle words." The Greek word for *mercy* is *eleonen,* from which we derive the English word *eleemosynary.* I don't recall ever using that word, but it's in the dictionary! It is an adjective used to describe the support of charitable organizations. Dropping coins into the Salvation Army kettle at Christmastime is a small eleemosynary act. The gift of mercy goes far beyond that. If you really like to do charitable work, God has almost certainly entrusted you with the gift of mercy.

The mobilization of the gifts of hospitality and mercy will be a significant issue when Christ judges the work of the church.

Read Matthew 25:34-36. Circle the "I was" phrase that speaks to the gift of hospitality. Underline the "I was" phrases that speak to the gift of mercy.

The stranger needs the ministry of hospitality. Those who are hungry, thirsty, poorly clothed, sick, or imprisoned need the loving ministry of someone with the gift of mercy.

You've probably already figured out that there may be some similarities between the gifts of hospitality and mercy. Notice that if you remove the *ity* from *hospitality* you get *hospital.* The word is derived from the Latin word *hospes.* When you hear the word *hospice* today, you usually think of an organization or place that

According to the grace given to us, we have different gifts: If prophecy, use it according to the standard of faith; if service, in service; if teaching, in teaching; if exhorting, in exhortation; giving, with generosity; leading, with diligence; showing mercy, with cheerfulness (Rom. 12:6-8).

The King will say to those on His right, "Come, you who are blessed by My Father, inherit the kingdom prepared for you from the foundation of the world. For I was hungry and you gave Me something to eat; I was thirsty and you gave Me something to drink; I was a stranger and you took Me in; I was naked and you clothed Me; I was sick and you took care of Me; I was in prison and you visited Me" (Matt. 25:34-36).

51

helps terminally ill persons experience maximum comfort, dignity, and family contact in the final days of their lives. Originally, *hospes* meant *a house or institution for guests*. Monks and other religious orders operated the first of these, caring for sick and wounded travelers, the aged, the poor, the disabled, and young homeless children. Orphanages, nursing homes, first-aid stations, rest stops, asylums, shelters, and soup kitchens historically fit under the umbrella term *hospital*. Wherever Christianity spreads, people groups and governments increasingly value, demand, and fund hospitals.

Hotels, motels, and restaurants consider their businesses part of the hospitality industry. Some of these companies have ventured into the arenas of retirement housing and long-term or nursing care for older adults. Many of the largest hospitals and mental health facilities are now commercial enterprises. This is not a negative reflection on the church but a positive one. A significant measurement of Christianity's impact on a society is how much the values of hospitality and mercy have been incorporated into that culture. Don't worry, though! There are always new groups whose needs are not being met by government or corporate organizations. It is to "the least of these" that Christ calls those with the gift of mercy to minister.

Even in a for-profit hospital, there is always the need for mercy showers at the bedside of the ill. In fact, hospital visitation is one of the best places to try out the gift of mercy. Vocationally, the gift of mercy can be the motivation for Christian chaplains, social workers, or physical therapists.

It is to "the least of these" that Christ calls those with the gift of mercy to minister.

Certain characteristics are common to the gift of mercy. Many also apply to the gift of hospitality. Check those below that describe you. Print the initials in the margin of anyone else who comes to your mind when you read the descriptions.

❏ Go beyond feeling compassion to practical actions that relieve the immediate suffering or make a person feel more comfortable.

❏ Put more value on deeds than words. Don't say, "Call if I can do something." Do something! Offer, "Would you rather have a meal the night you get home or the next night?" Or "I'm going to pick up your kids from school. What time would you like me to bring them home?"

❏ Don't worry about being paid back. The mercy shower often aids people who could never return the favor.

❏ Don't keep score. Never keep track of how many cakes they have baked, how many meals they have organized, or how many times the class meeting has been at their house.

- ❑ **Attracted to outsiders.** Distinguish the gifts of mercy and hospitality from serving and helps, for example, whose primary comfort zone is within the existing circle of fellowship.
- ❑ **Enjoy short-term ministry opportunities.** Often good at remembering names, faces, and details about people's children, jobs, background, etc. Have lots of acquaintances and enjoy calling a lot of people friends.
- ❑ **Empathize deeply with hurting persons.** Compelled to provide some type of immediate aid.

Normally, most of us respond to requests in one of three ways. We give people (1) what they deserve, (2) what they want, or (3) what they need. Prophets are prone to let people get what they deserve. Those with the gift of mercy are experts at dealing with the undeserving. But sometimes they tend to give people what they want, to relieve the immediate pain, without consideration for their long-term needs. People with the gift of mercy need to partner with people who have other gifts to ensure that needs are addressed. For example, in the case of financial needs, exhorters make excellent follow-up partners in ministries built around the gift of mercy. The person with the gift of mercy hates to say no. That's why most benevolent ministries need a person with the gift of administration who can do the unpleasant task of turning people away when resources are low or the client is abusing the system.

Spiritual gifts seldom operate best in isolation. It's a team thing! Church leaders should be careful about organizing ministries exclusively around one spiritual gift. An evangelism team, for example, needs administrators to keep everything organized, servants and helpers to prepare the information, and exhorters to follow up with new converts. A football team cannot win the Super Bowl with only a good quarterback. It must have a balance of talented linemen, backs, receivers, and defenders. In fact, it can't succeed with just the men on the field! It takes coaches and managers and helpers of all sorts behind the scenes. Sometimes a trainer is needed to provide a drink of water for the warriors or to bandage or tape up the wounded. On the church team those are the members with the gift of mercy.

> Spiritual gifts seldom operate best in isolation.

Describe a time when someone has shown mercy to you.

_____

DAY 4
The Gift of Evangelism

Jesus came near and said to them, "All authority has been given to Me in heaven and on earth. Go, therefore, and make disciples of all nations, baptizing them in the name of the Father and of the Son and of the Holy Spirit, teaching them to observe everything I have commanded you. And remember, I am with you always, to the end of the age" (Matt. 28:18-20).

He opened their minds to understand the Scriptures. He also said to them, "This is what is written: the Messiah would suffer and rise from the dead the third day, and repentance for forgiveness of sins would be proclaimed in His name to all the nations, beginning at Jerusalem. You are witnesses of these things" (Luke 24:45-48).

You will receive power when the Holy Spirit has come upon you, and you will be My witnesses in Jerusalem, in all Judea and Samaria, and to the ends of the earth (Acts 1:8).

Read the Great Commission passages—Matthew 28:18-20, Luke 24:4-48, and Acts 1:8—and determine if witnessing is a responsibility Jesus gave to all Christians or only those with the gift of evangelism.

Did you say a hearty "Amen!" to these verses? Maybe God has given you the gift of evangelism.

All Christians should be witnesses and receive training to witness effectively. Gifted evangelists are especially good at actually bringing people to the point of making an initial decision to become disciples of Jesus and members of His body, the church. Witnessing is a matter of faithfulness. The gift of evangelism is measured by effectiveness. In God's spiritual economy the effectiveness of evangelists in reaping a soul for the kingdom is certainly related to the faithfulness of those who preceded them by sowing and watering in that person's life through words of witness along the way.

If you wanted to learn to teach better, who would you want to train you? Someone with the gift of teaching. If you want to learn how to witness better, who would you want to train you? Of course, someone with the gift of evangelism! The best way to learn to lead someone to Christ is to see someone led to Him. That is why it is so important to have people with the gift of evangelism involved in training others. Whether your church uses one of LifeWay's evangelism-training solutions (*Share Jesus Without Fear, Life on Mission,* or FAITH Evangelism®) or another witness-training program, the mobilization of gifted evangelists in training others is crucial to effective outreach.

Certain characteristics are common among those with the gift of evangelism. Check those below that describe you. Print the initials of anyone else who comes to your mind as you read the descriptions.

❑ Primary motivation is to reach new people for Christ.
❑ Specialty is "spiritual obstetrics"–helping people be born again. Sometimes accused of not caring about discipleship. In reality they would just prefer to turn the new babe in Christ over to an exhorter or shepherd-teacher who specializes in "spiritual pediatrics" as soon

as possible. We'll look at the gifts of exhortation and shepherding next week.

❑ Sometimes sound like prophets, but when they talk about sin and repentance, they never stop there. Their primary message is the forgiveness of sin, the freedom from guilt, and the chance at a fresh start available in Jesus Christ. They live up to the word translated *evangelist,* which comes from a root that means *good news.*

❑ Really rather sympathetic to sinners and tolerant of their weaknesses. Often prefer to be around secular people than religious folks, especially if those religious folks seem unconcerned about the lost.

❑ Have a clear understanding of the gospel message, and often are able to memorize Scripture and gospel presentations.

❑ Experience a feeling of great joy when a person responds to an invitation to Christ. May applaud (or want to!) when someone is baptized.

One of my staff responsibilities at First Baptist Church, Garland, Texas, was to coordinate the counseling of people who made decisions during worship services. Three of the most faithful members of the decision counseling team were Betty, June, and Bill. Betty was excellent with people who had a nonevangelical religious background. June was particularly good at leading children to faith. Bill was wonderful with adults.

People were invited to respond in two ways: They could come down the aisle during the invitation, or they could make their way to the new member reception area after the service. Often I saw the joy on the faces of Bill, June, and others on the decision counseling team as I introduced them to an adult or young person who wanted to know more about Jesus or church membership. Their look told it all. They would rather be late to lunch than to miss such an opportunity. They had the gift of evangelism!

Although we will not study it in depth, some writers identify a gift of martyr, based on 1 Corinthians 13:3. Stephen was the first Christian martyr. (You can read about Stephen's ministry in Acts 6 and about his martyrdom in Acts 7.) Persons with the gift of martyr suffer for the faith in such a way that the work of Christ is advanced. Stephen's death had an impact on the eventual conversion of the Apostle Paul. A martyr's suffering is almost always the result of bold evangelism. The word *martyr* comes from the Greek *marturis,* which is the word translated "witnesses" in the Great Commission passages. Reread those passages.

Some writers identify a gift of martyr, based on 1 Corinthians 13:3.

We have said that there is a universal Christian responsibility corresponding to every spiritual gift. What might that be for the gift of martyr?

———————————————————————————
———————————————————————————
———————————————————————————

All Christians should strive to endure hardship and suffering without compromising their faith. In fact, it is often during the down times that a witness for Christ is the most powerful. The witness of a dying cancer patient to the love and care of God is remarkably powerful, for example.

Most Christians will never have to discover whether they have the gift of martyr. Many, however, could discover that they have the gift of evangelism. How? By trying it, of course! Timothy apparently did not have the gift of evangelism. Paul did not let the young pastor off the hook that easily but told him to "do the work of an evangelist" (2 Tim. 4:5).

Many with the gift of evangelism do not think it is a gift. Because of that position, they sometimes argue that everyone can be as effective at evangelism as they are. That's too bad because it robs God of some of the glory due Him as a result of their gift.

On the other hand, there are more people with the gift of evangelism in the church than practice it. You see, Satan hates the gift of evangelism. Discovering if you have it will not be easy work. The enemy will try to trick you, lie to you, distract you, discourage you, or anything else he can do to get you to quit before you can make that discovery. (A course like *Share Jesus Without Fear* would be a good starting point for anyone who wants to witness more effectively.)

Some church-growth authorities suggest that God has entrusted about 10 percent of the membership of any church with the gift of evangelism. Some argue that number is too low. The truth is that most pastors would be thrilled if just 5 percent of their members had discovered and were exercising the gift of evangelism.

What should a church do with the evangelists it identifies? I think they should do at least two things: (1) Leave them alone! Don't ask them to do any other jobs that detract from evangelism or evangelism training. (2) Make sure others know who they are so that they will always be able to say to someone to whom they are witnessing, "Would you mind talking with a friend of mine some more about this?"

As for you, keep a clear head about everything, endure hardship, do the work of an evangelist, fulfill your ministry (2 Tim. 4:5).

It is important to identify your spiritual gift. It is also important to identify the spiritual gifts of others. You need to understand all the spiritual gifts so you'll know whom to call for help when a situation requires gifts you don't have. Remember, being church is a team effort!

One of the best ministry teams I have ever observed operates Friendship House, a benevolent ministry of First Baptist Church, Garland, Texas. The ministry did not start as a church program conceived by the pastor or the denomination. It was born in the heart of a retired missionary, Ann (Mrs. Luther) Heath, and has grown to be one of the best known and loved ministries among the folks in the Garland community. Many other folks with similar gifts make Friendship House a model for a ministry of sharing.

When I was in Garland, the ministry was directed by Susan, to whom God has entrusted an incredible measure of the gift of mercy. Although not gifted in administration, Susan has learned a lot of administrative skills. She was helped a lot in that area by Sidney, who has the gift of administration. Sidney took care of a lot of the administrative details so Susan could interact with the clients.

Jim greeted folks when they came in. It can be frightening to go into a new place, especially if it is your first time to experience a crisis so severe that you must ask someone for help. Jim made the people feel welcome and helped put them at ease. He demonstrated the gift of hospitality.

Myrtle was a helper. She loved to be around Susan and would do anything Susan asked. What a blessing that was to Susan and the ministry of Friendship House.

There were a number of other people, many retired, who helped as well. Bill worked behind the scenes. He picked up day-old bread donated by the supermarket nearby. He, and a host of other men like him, repaired bicycles and furniture, using their gift of service.

Betty (yes, the same one you met earlier on the decision-counseling team!) helped round out that sharing ministry. Whenever appropriate, she took a few minutes to sit down with a client to share the good news of Jesus Christ.

Many dozens of folks have left Friendship House not only bound for home with groceries to feed their families but also bound for heaven, where one day they will experience neither hunger nor thirst. Betty has the gift of evangelism, that unique ability to engage people in such a way that they come to a point of decision for or against Jesus Christ.

It is important to identify your spiritual gift. It is also important to identify the spiritual gifts of others.

Ask God to bring to mind some of the folks in your church. Thank Him for the gifts He has given them. Ask Him to mold the gifts He has placed in your church into a powerful outreach for Christ in your community. List their names and their gifts. Be observant and add to your list until many gifts are represented. Pray for your fellow workers in Christ.

Name   **Gift**

_____

_____

_____

_____

_____

_____

_____

_____

_____

_____

_____

_____

_____

_____

_____

_____

_____

_____

_____

_____

_____

_____

_____

_____

_____

_____

_____

DAY 5

The Gift of Apostleship

Some biblical scholars argue that the need for—and thus the gift of—apostle expired with the completion of God's written Word, the Bible. In the technical sense of including only the twelve disciples, the office of apostle ceased when they died. The twelve spoke with unusual authority. After all, they had lived with the Lord Jesus, been taught by Him, witnessed His resurrection, and personally received His commission. Their names will be written on the foundation of the New Jerusalem (Rev. 21:14). In this restricted sense there are certainly no more "big A" apostles!

But the New Testament also uses the word *apostle* in a more general sense to describe those who were affirmed by the church and given authority to start new work or strengthen exist-ing work—often in a different culture or in multiple cultures. Barnabas, James the brother of Jesus, Silas, Timothy, and most notably Paul were all called apostles.

The Greek word transliterated *apostle* means *one sent*. The Latin word transliterated *missionary* means the same thing. The gift of apostleship is the God-given capacity to exercise extraordinary authority in the establishment and development of churches, especially new ones, often in the face of cultural barriers.

The gift of apostleship is the gift God has given to effective church planters and missionaries. It is also sometimes applied to the leaders of organizations or mission boards whose mission is to start or strengthen churches.

Some time ago I had the privilege to interact with a group of new directors of missions from across the United States. These men lead the cooperative work of churches in a particular geographi-cal area, usually spanning one or more counties. The organization is called an association. In some places the leaders are still called associational missionaries. There were two characteristics common to every director I met. He loved his churches and desired for them to be strong and effective. I saw it in John's eyes when I asked him, "Do you love your churches?" His watery eyes only confirmed his verbal response. God has entrusted him with several gifts. He will be effective not only because of those gifts but mostly because God has unmistakably bestowed on him the gift of apostleship.

The gift of apostleship is almost always exercised in concert with other spiritual gifts.

The gift of apostleship is almost always exercised in concert with other spiritual gifts. The characteristics of the gift are perhaps best understood in comparison to other gifts.

Below check the boxes of the characteristics that might describe you. In the margin print the initials of anyone else who comes to mind from the descriptions.

❑ Have the ability to adapt to new languages and cultures. On the domestic front church planters will almost always have to adapt to new customs and perhaps differences in speech. On the international field this will usually involve learning a new language as well as customs.

❑ Show interest in witnessing the birth of a brand-new group of believers who have never been effectively reached by the message of the gospel, often seen in a missionary or a church planter with the gift of apostleship.

❑ Easily turn the new work over to gifted shepherd-teachers who will take a long-term responsibility for the welfare and growth of the new flock.

❑ With the added gift of mercy, might work in a foreign country in a social ministry or in a Christian relief or health-care mission.

❑ With the added gift of teaching, might help establish a school in an international location. Schools have long been a proven strategy both to improve a society and to teach people about Christ.

❑ With the added gift of administration or leadership, might help organize the central business functions of a missions organization overseas.

❑ With the added gift of of serving or helps, might be involved in agricultural missions, helping a tribal people learn to use their water and soil resources in more productive, healthy ways.

❑ Have a unique affinity for meeting strangers. It is not at all uncommon for the missionary team to include at least one person who has the gift of hospitality.

Do any of these ideas tug at your heart? Describe your feelings.

_____
_____
_____

Do they describe anyone else you know? Whom?

_____
_____

If you believe God may have given you the gift of apostleship, you should probably do a couple of things to check it out:

1. Take part in a mission trip! This is a wonderful opportunity to try out the gift of apostleship.

2. Contact a missionary-appointing agency such as the North American Mission Board or the International Mission Board. It will have persons who are qualified to help you discern whether God has gifted and equipped you to be an effective church planter or missionary.

Read Romans 15:20 and 2 Corinthians 10:16, both written by the apostle Paul, to discover another key characteristic of a person with the gift of apostleship. Is the person with the gift of apostleship a pathfinder or a trailblazer?

_____

_____

_____

The person with the gift of apostleship is a trailblazer, preferring to work in new places, among new peoples, or to oversee the work of an expanding area of influence.

What do you think is the universal, as-you-go responsibility for all Christians in the area of apostleship?

_____

_____

_____

Did you say something like learning about missions, praying for missionaries, or staying informed about missions? Every day thousands of Southern Baptists pray for missionaries on their birthdays using the guide in the devotional magazine *Open Windows*. *On Mission!* magazine provides colorful photos and wonderful stories of the work of the North American Mission Board. Ask your pastor or a staff member how to secure copies of these magazines.

Did Jesus have the gift of apostleship? He was sent. He went willingly. He came to a place with plenty of cultural barriers. He started the church. He continues to care deeply about the church He started. Yes, Jesus is the supreme example of the gift of apostleship too!

My aim is to evangelize where Christ has not been named, in order that I will not be building on someone else's foundation (Rom. 15:20).

... so that we may preach the gospel to the regions beyond you, not boasting about what has already been done in someone else's area of ministry (2 Cor. 10:16).

If you have a prayer list of missionaries, bring their names before the Father right now. If not, ask God to bring some nation to your mind, and pray for the missionaries He has called to serve there.

Using either the Internet—International Mission Board *(www.imb. org)*, North American Mission Board *(www.namb.net)*—or the devotional periodicals mentioned, discover a ministry that is new to you. Make notes about it here. Pray for the missionaries and for people in that area who are reached by this ministry.

Gifts That Ground Us in God's Word

This week you will—

- grow in your appreciation for the speaking gifts that ground us in God's Word;
- understand the gift of prophecy and its role in the church today;
- understand the gift of exhortation and how easy it is to try it;
- understand the differences and similarities between the teaching and shepherding gifts.

Gifts That Speak Through More than Speech

Do you enjoy studying the Bible? Are you prone to interpret world events, everyday situations, and just about everything in between in terms of how God's Word might apply? Do you enjoy talking about what God is showing you in His Word? Are you compelled to believe that the starting point for addressing the problems of the world, the church, the family, and individual lives is to understand and obey what God says about the subject in the Bible? Are you convinced that the Bible is God's commentary on human life? Do you feel burdened to share God's commentary with others?

If you answered yes to any of these questions, God may have entrusted you with one of the four speaking gifts. But even if He has not, you need to understand how these four gifts operate within the church and how you should relate to them.

These gifts can be expressed in ways other than speech. Although most people with these gifts are talkers, some people with these gifts communicate through writing, music, art, drama, or some other expressive way. What distinguishes these folks from others with similar talents is the content and concern of what they communicate. These gifts are devoted to the Bible and have a strong desire to communicate the truths it teaches. The greatest joy of those with these gifts is to see others respond to God in love, trust, and obedience.

In Ephesians 3:17-19 Paul prayed for some early believers that they would be grounded in their faith. Speaking gifts could also be called grounding gifts because their main effect is to ground God's people in God's Word.

This Week's Key Verse
You are the body of Christ, and individual members of it (1 Cor. 12:27).

This Week's Lessons
Day 1: The Speaking Gifts
Day 2: The Gift of Prophecy
Day 3: The Gift of Exhortation
Day 4: The Gift of Teaching
Day 5: The Gift of Shepherding

I pray that you, being rooted and firmly established ["grounded," KJV] in love, may be able to comprehend with all the saints what is the breadth and width, height and depth, and to know the Messiah's love that surpasses knowledge, so you may be filled with all the fullness of God (Eph. 3:17-19).

The Speaking Gifts

The spiritual gifts of prophecy, teaching, exhortation, and shepherding were critical to the growth and survival of the first-century church. They continue to be absolutely essential to the church today.

Scan each of Paul's three main teachings about spiritual gifts. Place a check beside the passages that include gifts related to prophesying or teaching:
____ Romans 12
____ 1 Corinthians 12
____ Ephesians 4

All three of Paul's major teachings about spiritual gifts include references to prophets, prophecy, or prophesying, as well as teachers, teaching, or pastor-teachers. Before the New Testament was completed and circulated, the role of these gifts was especially important. Their role was foundational in proclaiming and explaining "the mystery of the gospel" (Eph. 6:19).

Paul explained to Timothy that those who preach and teach God's Word do so with a variety of results in mind.

Read 2 Timothy 3:16-17 and 2 Timothy 4:2-3. Underline the different reasons people need to hear God's Word.

God's people need to hear God's Word whenever they need *teaching* in the ways of God, *rebuking* in regard to their behavior, *correcting* when they have wrong ideas or attitudes, *training* in how to relate to God and other people, and when they need to be *encouraged* to continue to walk the path of faith.

Churches should be structured to maximize the gifts that ground the body of Christ in the Word of God. This became apparent when the early church was but a few months old. In Acts 2–4 we read about the remarkable way in which the first church members shared with one another. By Acts 6 the apostles were already spending time trying to deal with folks who thought they were not getting their fair share. Read in Acts 6:2-4 the solution they found.

Pray also for me, that the message may be given to me when I open my mouth to make known with boldness the mystery of the gospel (Eph. 6:19).

All Scripture is inspired by God and is profitable for teaching, for rebuking, for correcting, for training in righteousness, so that the man of God may be complete, equipped for every good work (2 Tim. 3:16-17).

Proclaim the message; persist in it whether convenient or not; rebuke, correct, and encourage with great patience and teaching. For the time will come when they will not tolerate sound doctrine, but according to their own desires, will accumulate teachers for themselves because they have an itch to hear something new (2 Tim. 4:2-3).

The Twelve summoned the whole company of the disciples and said, "It would not be right for us to give up preaching about God to wait on tables. Therefore,

These seven men are often considered the first deacons. What might their spiritual gifts have been? _____

_____

As a result of these men exercising their gifts, what important duties did the apostles have more time to do? _____

_____

Certainly these seven had demonstrated that they had a gift of wisdom. They probably also had the gift of service. The Greek word translated "serving" is *diakonos,* from which we get the English word *deacon.* If these were indeed the first deacons, you would hope they had that gift! Some perhaps also had the gift of administration. In Acts 6–7 we read how one of these seven, Stephen, also demonstrated gifts of miracles and prophecy. Another of the seven, Philip, also discovered he had the gift of evangelism.

In Acts 8:26-40 how did Philip demonstrate the principle of going out of your way to exercise the spiritual gift of evangelism?

_____

_____

Philip went way out of his way to share Christ with the Ethiopian official! He, like Stephen, became a bold preacher of the gospel.

What about the other five? Prochorus, Nicanor, Timon, Parmenas, and Nicolaus apparently continued to do the work of service behind the scenes, in accordance with their gifts. As a result, the apostles could spend a maximum amount of time on the important work of praying and preparing to preach and teach. Blessed is the church that has folks who will do the behind-the-scenes work so that others might give adequate time to studying the Scriptures and seeking God's message for His people!

The stories of Stephen and Philip point to another important principle about discovering spiritual gifts: A willingness to serve is almost always the starting line in the journey to discover your spiritual gift(s). There is really only one way to know for sure whether God has given you any particular gift:

1. Get involved wholeheartedly in a ministry where one of your possible gifts would be useful.
2. Examine your feelings—with *joy,* not *easy* as your criterion!
3. Evaluate your effectiveness.
4. Listen for confirmation (or lack of it!) from others in the body.

brothers, select from among you seven men of good reputation, full of the Spirit and wisdom, whom we can appoint to this duty. But we will devote ourselves to prayer and to the preaching ministry" (Acts 6:2-4).

An angel of the Lord spoke to Philip: "Get up and go south to the road that goes down from Jerusalem to desert Gaza." So he got up and went. There was an Ethiopian man, a eunuch and high official of Candace, queen of the Ethiopians, who was in charge of her entire treasury. He had come to worship in Jerusalem and was sitting in his chariot on his way home, reading the prophet Isaiah aloud. The Spirit told Philip, "Go and join that chariot." When Philip ran up to it, he heard him reading the prophet Isaiah, and said, "Do you understand what you're reading?" "How can I," he said, "unless someone guides me?" So he invited Philip to come up and sit with him. ... So Philip proceeded to tell him the good news about Jesus, beginning from that Scripture (Acts 8:26-31,35).

Even those with one of the grounding gifts most often discover those gifts after they have passed the test of serving. Many excellent Sunday School teachers started as faithful care group leaders. In their service they discovered that they had some characteristics common to those who have been entrusted with the grounding gifts.

Below check the common characteristics of the grounding gifts that sound like you! In the margin print the initials of anyone else who comes to mind.

❑ They believe the Bible is God's Word and completely true and trustworthy.

❑ They almost always prefer to be the speaker in church groups.

❑ They generally have an accurate self-image and often a strong personality.

❑ Their lifestyle validates their message—and when it does not, they are hard on themselves and feel a deep sense of guilt and conviction.

Did you check three or more? Maybe God has entrusted you with one of the speaking gifts. What about the rest of us? Read Acts 17:11 to see what one group of early Christians did.

According to Acts 17:11, should those without the speaking gifts leave Bible study to those who have these gifts?

_____

The people ... welcomed the message with eagerness and examined the Scriptures daily to see if these things were so (Acts 17:11).

These gifts guide us in understanding God's Word, and we listen with eagerness. But we should also know for ourselves what the Bible says. Eagerness and examination—pretty good ways to relate to those with the gifts of prophecy, teaching, exhortation, and shepherding. We'll look more closely at each of these gifts over the next four days.

DAY 2
The Gift of Prophecy

No spiritual gift is unimportant. But some are more important for the work of the church as a whole than others (see 1 Cor. 14). The problem in the Corinthian church was that some were exalting members who exhibited the gift of tongues as being somehow more spiritual than the other members. They were also apparently frowning upon the gift of prophecy.

Scan 1 Corinthians 14. Which gift did Paul indicate was more important to the growth and health of the church?

_____

Paul said that 5 words of prophecy were more valuable than 10,0000 words in tongues. He introduced the chapter by declaring that the gift of prophecy should be especially desired in the church. The verb is plural, indicating that the church as a whole should seek and call out those with this important gift. Although Paul did not forbid speaking in tongues, his teaching is clear that it should be carefully limited in public gatherings. Prophecy, on the other hand, should have a prominent place when God's people come together for worship.

Today this gift is primarily associated with powerful preaching. But all preachers don't have the gift of prophecy. And all persons with the gift of prophecy are not preachers—at least vocationally! Most of those who have this gift are, however, used to hearing other people say, "Don't start preaching at me!"

Read Acts 2:14-18. Put a checkmark beside those people who Peter indicates will prophesy because of the Holy Spirit's coming at Pentecost:

___ Men	___ Women
___ Young people	___ Old people

All persons who are in Christ are eligible for the gift of prophecy. In fact, Peter is probably not referring to the gift of prophecy at all in this passage. He is more likely saying, "From now on, don't be surprised to hear any believer prophesy." Remember that every spiritual gift has an every Christian, an along-the-way counterpart.

According to the grace given to us, we have different gifts: If prophecy, use it according to the standard of faith (Rom. 12:6).

Peter stood up with the Eleven, raised his voice, and proclaimed to them: "Jewish men and all you residents of Jerusalem, let this be known to you and pay attention to my words. For these people are not drunk, as you suppose, since it's only nine in the morning. On the contrary, this is what was spoken through the prophet Joel: And it will be in the last days, says God, that I will pour out My Spirit on all humanity; then your sons and your daughters will prophesy, your young men will see visions, and your old men will dream dreams. I will even pour out My Spirit on My male and female slaves in those days, and they will prophesy (Acts 2:14-18).

Those who are gifted have a special capacity in that area. This is true of prophecy, too. All of us should be ready to preach the Word when an opportunity presents itself as we go. But some have a special gift of prophecy, a gift they go out of their way to exercise.

The message of the Old Testament prophets usually included one or more of these basic points:

1. An analysis of the current situation from God's perspective
2. The consequences of continuing in that path
3. The need for change/repentance
4. The promise of God's grace and restoration if the change in direction was made

The message was at least as much prescriptive as predictive.

Prophecy does not usually involve *foretelling*—predicting the future—as much as it does *forthtelling*—forcefully speaking the truth. The word *proclaim* is perhaps a better word than *preach* to describe what a person with the gift of prophecy does. Typically, the ministry of the prophet is a public one. Ironically, a prophet's ministry often feels like a lonely one. Prophets are more sponta neous than teachers and less studious! They are less comfortable one on one or in a small group than the exhorter. Unlike the shepherd, who prefers to know everybody in the group on a first-name basis, the prophet prefers speaking to a large crowd. In fact, the larger the crowd, the better—even if it means going on television or radio to get the message out. Many vocational evangelists actually exhibit the gift of prophecy in their preaching.

Some other typical characteristics of those with the gift of prophecy are listed below. Put a checkmark beside those that might describe you. Also think about others you know who might fit these descriptions. Print their initials in the margin.

❑ Tuned in to how God views situations, especially if evil or hypocrisy is present.

❑ Issues-oriented; usually have an opinion about everything! Not fearful to tackle the tough issues.

❑ Proclaim God's truth with passion, even if they must do so alone.

❑ Tend to see everything as black-and-white, right or wrong.

❑ Message is one of urgency; tend to expect an immediate decision or response. (Repent now!)

❑ Like the Old Testament prophets, speak with the conviction: "Thus saith the Lord."

❑ Don't worry too much about what others will think about what they say.

The person who prophesies speaks to people for edification, encouragement, and consolation (1 Cor. 14:3).

It follows that speaking in other languages is intended as a sign, not to believers but to unbelievers. But prophecy is not for unbelievers but for believers (1 Cor. 14:22).

❑ Deeply concerned about the reputation of the church.
❑ Quick to give advice; sometimes impatient with people and their problems.
❑ Speak with authority, especially about the Bible.
❑ Sometimes viewed as negative; have to work hard to be positive.
❑ Often accused of talking too much but just can't seem to help it!

If you checked a number of these characteristics, God may have entrusted you with the spiritual gift of prophecy. Or maybe the list brought others to mind, and thinking of them helps you understand them better. You will want to pray for an opportunity to share this in a way that affirms them and their gift.

First Corinthians 14 gives some guidelines for how the gift of prophecy is supposed to function in the church and how we should relate to those who prophesy.

1. What are three ways the prophet helps the church (v. 3)? He/she

_____

_____, and _____

2. According to verse 22, prophecy is intended primarily for (check one): ___ believers ___ unbelievers

3. What might happen if an unbeliever hears the words of a prophet (vv. 23-25)? _____

_____

4. What controls should the gathered church implement in regard to the public expression of the gift of prophecy (vv. 29-32)?
   • _____
   • _____
   • _____

The prophet *edifies* (builds up), *encourages* (exhorts), and *consoles* (comforts). The prophetic message is incomplete if it stops short of these goals. It is intended primarily for believers, though an unbeliever who hears the preaching might come under conviction and acknowledge God's presence. Paul encouraged the Corinthians to have an orderly worship experience, where no more than two or three proclaimed a prophetic word.

Paul urged the listeners to check out the message carefully. Many cult leaders claim a direct revelation from God contrary

If the whole church assembles together, and all are speaking in other languages, and people who are uninformed or unbelievers come in, will they not say that you are out of your minds? But if all are prophesying, and some unbeliever or uninformed person comes in, he is convicted by all and is judged by all. The secrets of his heart will be revealed, and as a result he will fall down on his face and worship God, proclaiming, "God is really among you" (1 Cor. 14:23-25).

Two or three prophets should speak, and the others should evaluate. But if something has been revealed to another person sitting there, the first prophet should be silent. For you can all prophesy one by one, so that everyone may learn and everyone may be encouraged. And the prophets' spirits are under the control of the prophets (1 Cor. 14:29-32).

Paul taught that a person with a spiritual gift has the ability to exercise control over that gift.

to Scripture yet are able to gather around themselves those who blindly follow.

Finally, Paul taught that a person with a spiritual gift has the ability to exercise control over that gift. *The Living Bible* paraphrases verse 32: "Remember that a person who has a message from God has the power to stop himself or wait his turn." Self-control is a fruit of the Holy Spirit, after all. The self-control principle is true of every spiritual gift. Your spiritual gift should never be an excuse for inappropriate, uncontrolled, or untimely behavior.

Thank God for those who have influenced your life positively through preaching or some other prophetic ministry. Pledge to exercise self-control in using your spiritual gift(s).

DAY 3

The Gift of Exhortation

From yesterday's study you recall that exhortation is an element of prophecy. It is an important aspect of the other two grounding gifts too. But exhortation is also a spiritual gift in its own right.

What if you were an obstetrician on an airplane and someone was having a heart attack? Would you refuse to help because you weren't a heart specialist? Hopefully, you would provide whatever assistance you could until a cardiologist could take over. That's the along-the-way principle we've mentioned so often already. That principle certainly applies to the gift of exhortation. All Christians should seek to be encouragers. There are some folks, however, who are especially equipped by God with a gift of exhortation.

Joseph was a Levite (priest) from Cyprus, and a member of the first church in Jerusalem. He is first mentioned in Acts 4:36-37. The gift of exhortation was so apparent with Joseph that the apostles gave him the name _____, which means "Son of _____."

Barnabas really was a "son of encouragement." If you were going to be called a name, that is a good one to be called. His story began with an act of generosity, but it didn't end there. When the church was reluctant to believe that Saul, the persecutor of the church, had become Paul the believer, guess who was there to vouch for him? Barnabas. When the first Gentile church started at Antioch, guess who encouraged them? Barnabas. When that church needed a preacher, guess who recruited Paul for the job? Barnabas. When Paul started on the first missionary journey, guess who was at his side? Barnabas. When Paul became disappointed with John Mark, guess who stuck up for and restored Mark? Barnabas!

Like Barnabas, the gift of exhortation is less public than that of prophecy. After all, you don't hear about too many TV exhorters! Unlike the prophet or teacher, the gifted exhorter usually operates most effectively in one-on-one or small-group settings.

The word translated "exhortation" is a form of the word *paraclete*, the word Jesus used (John 14:16) when He revealed the coming of the Holy Spirit as Comforter and Counselor. The word literally means *one who is called alongside to help*. The effective

According to the grace given to us, we have different gifts: If prophecy, use it according to the standard of faith; if service, in service; if teaching, in teaching; if exhorting, in exhortation (Rom. 12:6-8).

Joseph, a Levite and a Cypriot by birth, whom the apostles named Barnabas, which is translated Son of Encouragement, sold a field he owned, brought the money, and laid it at the apostles' feet (Acts 4:36-37).

exhorter really is like the Holy Spirit with skin. It is a dual role. One is the comforting role, but the other is the counseling role.

What do you think of when you think of a counselor? Certainly, an effective counselor is a good listener. He or she shows empathy and understanding. But an effective counselor almost never just stops with "It's OK. You're OK." Godly counselors almost always encourage the client with a plan of action for moving forward to greater emotional and spiritual health.

Counselor is also used to refer to the work of an attorney. In 1 John 2:1 Jesus is called our Advocate, one who speaks to the Father in our defense. The word is *paraclete*.

Barnabas was in the role of defense attorney when he endorsed Paul to the early church. But the gift of exhortation also includes a prosecuting attorney role. The gifted exhorter knows when we need to be admonished or challenged. Unlike the prophet, however, he or she is more likely to do so in private, coming alongside us for our own good.

Coach would be a good modern word to describe the gifted exhorter. Good coaches have an uncanny ability to know when to get in a player's face, when to give an understanding pat on the back when a player has messed up, when to show a player a better way to execute the plays, and when to help players develop the skills of their position. Does that sound like anyone you know?

My little children, I am writing you these things so that you may not sin. But if anyone does sin, we have an advocate with the Father—Jesus Christ the righteous One (1 John 2:1).

Some other typical characteristics of those with the gift of exhortation are listed below. Put a checkmark by those that might describe you. Also think about others you know who might fit these descriptions. Print their initials in the margin.

❑ Big on application. A biblical pragmatist. Believe that Bible truth works in the lives of believers.

❑ May prefer topical studies over verse-by-verse exposition.

❑ Delight in showing individuals *how* to change, whereas the prophet's goal is to get people to *decide* to change.

❑ Feel comfortable in small groups or one on one (more so than the other grounding gifts).

❑ Prefer dialogue and discussion rather than lecturing.

❑ Prefer to help you work it out for yourself than just to tell you what to do or believe.

❑ A spiritual cheerleader. Desire to cheer on believers to walk in faith, whatever circumstances they face.

❑ Won't just tell you everything is going to be OK. Will stay with you to work out a plan of action.

- ❑ Will stick with you during difficult circumstances to help you be strong and remain faithful to the Lord.
- ❑ *Potential* is a key word for the exhorter. Perceive potential in people who want to grow spiritually. See potential for growth even in times of testing. Romans 8:28 is a favorite verse!
- ❑ More person centered than the teacher. More patient than the prophet. Less patient than the shepherd with people who don't show progress. Likely to challenge persons either to get with the program or make room for somebody else!
- ❑ Often express their gift in writing as well as speaking. May write terrific notes and letters of encouragement.

Encouragers Wanted

The Book of Hebrews was written to Jewish Christians living in suburban Rome. Well, really they were hiding out there! You see, the Roman emperor Nero was on the warpath, and many Christians were being persecuted—even tortured—for calling Jesus Lord. Times were tough. Some were considering revoking their Christian faith and lifestyle. It was legal to be a Jew, illegal to be a Christian. What a great time to receive an encouraging letter.

In Hebrews 10:23-25 what did the writer exhort the readers to do?
1. Hold on to _____ .
2. Promote _____ .
3. Not staying away from _____ ...
4. But _____ (same word as *exhort*)
   one another!

If this passage in Hebrews really appeals to you and if you checked a number of the characteristics above, God may have entrusted you with the spiritual gift of exhortation. You like to encourage people to hold on to the faith, to spur them on to love and good deeds, to make a habit of meeting together, and to encourage one another. Of course, you can't really know for sure about your gift until you get involved in a ministry that requires it. What's especially great about trying out the gift of exhortation is that you can't mess up! People all around us are in need of a word of exhortation. Some of those people might even live in your own house.

Read 1 Thessalonians 2:11-12. Ask God to make you that kind of encourager along the way and especially in your own home.

We know that all things work together for the good of those who love God: those who are called according to His purpose (Rom. 8:28).

Let us hold on to the confession of our hope without wavering, for He who promised is faithful. And let us be concerned about one another in order to promote love and good works, not staying away from our meetings, as some habitually do, but encouraging each other, and all the more as you see the day drawing near (Heb. 10:23-25).

Like a father with his own children, we encouraged, comforted, and implored each one of you to walk worthy of God, who calls you into His own kingdom and glory (1 Thess. 2:11-12).

DAY 4
The Gift of Teaching

According to the grace given to us, we have different gifts: If prophecy, use it according to the standard of faith; if service, in service; if teaching, in teaching (Rom. 12:6-8).

God has placed these in the church: first apostles, second prophets, third teachers, next, miracles, then gifts of healing, helping, managing, various kinds of languages (1 Cor. 12:28).

Do not be conformed to this age, but be transformed by the renewing of your mind, so that you may discern what is the good, pleasing, and perfect will of God (Rom. 12:2).

What you have heard from me in the presence of many witnesses, commit to faithful men who will be able to teach others also (2 Tim. 2:2).

Jesus has every spiritual gift. In His earthly ministry He was referred to as Teacher (Rabbi) more often than Preacher or Prophet. It shouldn't be surprising then that there are more teachers than preachers in the body of Christ. Whereas prophets are proclaimers, teachers are explainers. Whereas prophets tend to be emotional, teachers tend to be more cerebral. Whereas the prophet desires a change in the way you feel and an exhorter in the way you act, the teacher desires a change in the way you think. Like the prophet, teachers don't mind speaking to a crowd. In fact, they may even get a little discouraged when only a few people show up to hear the fruit of their intense preparation.

The Greek word for this gift is *didaskalos*. It can be translated *master, teacher,* or *doctor*. Some churches use a master-teacher approach in their education ministry. A person with a highly developed gift of teaching will present the biblical material to a large group, followed by discussion in smaller groups led by those with gifts of exhortation or shepherding. It would not be unusual for that gifted teacher to be Dr. Somebody! But many gifted teachers have never earned a doctorate. That being said, they are absolutely dependent on those who have devoted their lives to biblical scholarship: studying and debating the precise meanings of Hebrew and Greek words; cataloguing and describing scriptural concepts; digging—sometimes literally—to determine the historical and cultural context of a Bible book; and capturing all of this knowledge in Bible concordances, dictionaries, encyclopedias, and atlases.

If you are a professional educator, you already noticed the similarity to the English word *didactic*. Any story, poem, drama, program, or presentation that intends to teach a truth or convey a message is didactic. Their desire is to get something into your head. A favorite verse is Romans 12:2. When you've been under the instruction of a gifted teacher, you'll find yourself saying things like, "Oh, now I get it," "Wow, I never saw that before," "Yeah, that's right," or, "Of course, that's so obvious now."

Perhaps like no other spiritual gift, those with the gift of teaching depend on gifted teachers who have gone before them. According to 2 Timothy 2:2, it is the responsibility of teachers to reproduce themselves. That's why gifted teachers are careful about sharing a new insight without checking to see if other teachers have reached similar conclusions.

According to Hebrews 5:12, do you think there is a universal Christian responsibility related to teaching?_____

Yes, all Christians have the responsibility to teach, especially in their own households. But God has given some a special giftedness and a special responsibility to be called teacher.

Some other typical characteristics of those with the gift of teaching are listed below. Put a checkmark beside those that describe you. Also think about others you know who might fit these descriptions. Print their initials in the margin.
❏ Can make profound things simple and vague things clear.
❏ Strive to organize biblical facts into an orderly, memorable system. Like to use tables and charts.
❏ Generally have an organized mind (but maybe not an organized desk).
❏ Demand accuracy. Really irritated when a biblical word or name is mispronounced or a verse is used out of context.
❏ Tend to think that if people have enough information they can make their own application.
❏ Like time alone to ponder, study, read, and/or write.
❏ Like to use good visual materials when teaching: posters, overhead cels, printed handouts, etc.
❏ Tolerate, at best, being interrupted with questions. Likely to say, "We'll save time at the end of the session for questions." Typically run out of time before any questions can be asked, unless really self-disciplined (but may feel pressured to cut out important information to have questions).

Does this sound like anybody you know? If it sounds like you, maybe God has given you the gift of teaching! Can you think of others you know who have the gift of teaching? Are they currently serving in a teaching responsibility?

Saying It in Song
Music is one of the most powerful mediums for expressing the gifts of teaching and exhortation. Music is not a spiritual gift in the strict sense since God has blessed all humankind through this wonderful medium. But the highest use of music is to help Christians learn, remember, and obey the truths of God's Word. Music is never more

Though by this time you ought to be teachers, you need someone to teach you again the basic principles of God's revelation. You need milk, not solid food (Heb. 5:12).

powerful than when used as a vehicle for the expression
of a spiritual gift.

Let the message about the Messiah dwell richly among you, teaching and admonishing one another in all wisdom, and singing psalms, hymns, and spiritual songs, with gratitude in your hearts to God (Col 3:16).

How does Colossians 3:16 relate music to grounding the body of Christ in God's Word?

_____

_____

What are some of your favorite psalms, hymns, or spiritual songs?

_____

_____

_____

_____

The Bible says that words put to music are a powerful means of helping God's people be grounded in the truths of God's Word. Songs and singers were an important part of Jewish culture and worship. That carried over into the Christian movement. One of my favorite hymns is "Hark! The Herald Angels Sing." I've always thought it unfortunate that we only sing it at Christmastime because Charles Wesley's words give an amazingly concise but thorough summary of the doctrine of Christ, including His pre-existence and incarnation. If you have the gift of teaching, you've probably already started looking for a hymnal to check that out!

Maybe you have other favorites. If you have the gift of evangelism, maybe you like invitation hymns like "Just as I Am" or songs like "People Need the Lord." Maybe you have the gift of prophecy and love to sing "Revive Us Again." If you like contemporary Christian music, you might have the gift of exhortation, since most of this popular music is of the encouragement genre. Maybe you have the gift of giving and hate it when the song leader leaves out the third verse of "Take My Life and Let It Be." (That's the "Take my silver and my gold, not a mite would I withhold" stanza!) Or maybe you love Psalm 23. Maybe you have the gift of shepherding. We'll look at that gift tomorrow!

If you have a hymnal at home, meditate on a favorite song. If not, meditate on Psalm 23.

DAY 5
The Gift of Shepherding

You'll remember that we are using the term *shepherding* to identify this gift, usually translated *pastor-teacher.* The Greek word for *pastor* is *poimen.* The other 16 times it appears in the New Testament, it is translated *shepherd,* so we are on solid ground doing so. The main idea is to make clear that the gift is not the same thing as the office or position of pastor in the local church. More people in the church have the gift of shepherd than just the pastor. In fact, the pastor and staff might have the position but not the gift!

The prophet prefers to speak from a pulpit. The teacher is comfortable behind a lectern. The shepherd, on the other hand, is most comfortable sitting down among the flock. Picture a shepherd with a staff, sitting or standing among the flock, watching for and warning of danger, using his staff to pull back in those who begin to stray away, and soothing and guiding the sheep with his voice, and you've got a pretty good idea about the gift of shepherding.

The gift of shepherding includes the responsibility of teaching but not at the same level as the gift of teaching. You can be a teacher without being a shepherd, but you can't be a shepherd without being a teacher. Shepherds teach, but they approach that part of their ministry a little differently than the teacher.

The distinguishing characteristic of the shepherding gift is a long-term perspective. Unlike the prophet, who expects immediate response, the shepherd is content to watch people make incremental progress. Unlike the exhorter, who doesn't really have much patience with someone who doesn't want to grow in the Lord, the shepherd stays in touch with even the chronic absentee. In fact, the shepherd often tends to pay more attention to straying or troubled sheep than faithful and healthy ones. Unlike the teacher, who may spend hours of preparation for a one-hour lesson, the shepherd studies just enough to feed the flock what they need.

Along with prophets and exhorters, shepherds are highly dependent on the work of gifted teachers who have written commentaries, compiled concordances, edited Bible dictionaries, systematized theology, researched word meanings, studied church history, etc. Shepherds don't spend a lot of time trying to be original. If a gifted teacher has put together some good spiritual food, the shepherd is quite pleased to feed it to her flock too!

He personally gave some to be apostles, some prophets, some evangelists, some pastors and teachers, for the training of the saints in the work of ministry, to build up the body of Christ, until we all reach unity in the faith and in the knowledge of God's Son (Eph. 4:11-13).

Does that mean shepherds are lazy? Not at all! Most would really like to spend more time in study and preparation. But their priorities are their people. Arranging a meal for a grieving member. Visiting someone in the hospital. Calling to chat with a prospective member. Checking with care group leaders to see if anyone needs attention. Shepherds are just more likely to run out of time to prepare than those with only the gift of teaching.

How can you tell the difference between two people with the gifts of teaching and shepherding? Ask this question: "What are you teaching right now in your church?" The person with the gift of teaching might respond something like this: "I am teaching a six-week course on the first 12 chapters of the Book of Genesis. I believe that's the foundation for understanding the Bible." The person with the gift of shepherding, on the other hand, is more likely to answer, "I'm teaching a class of seventh-grade boys again this year." He might even add with excitement in his voice, "One of them brought a friend a few weeks ago. He's going to be baptized this morning!"

Some other typical characteristics of those with the gift of shepherding are listed below. Put a checkmark by those that might describe you. Also think about others you know who might fit these descriptions. Print their initials in the margin.

❑ More likely to "cut 'em some slack" than the prophet or exhorter.
❑ Love people, protective of those in their care, and prone to jealousy if their flock feeds in someone else's pasture.
❑ Sensitive to problems in the flock that might cause disharmony.
❑ Remember names, faces, and voices well.
❑ Self-sacrificing to the extent that they sometimes neglect to involve the members of the group in ministry.
❑ Like to study but generally just enough to feed the flock what they need, generally one meal at a time. Saturday night preparation is a recurring reality.
❑ Draw people to themselves easily and give them up reluctantly!
❑ *Count* is an important word in the shepherd's vocabulary: "You can *count* on me." "Did you *count* how many were there?" "Don't *count* them out yet; I'm still working on them!"

Whom does this sound like? Maybe a beloved Sunday School teacher (currently or in your past)? Maybe you? If so, one of the best ministries in the church for those with the gift of shepherding is in the Sunday School (or your church's equivalent for small

I am the good shepherd. The good shepherd lays down his life for the sheep. The hired man, since he's not the shepherd and doesn't own the sheep, leaves them and runs away when he sees a wolf coming. The wolf then snatches and scatters them. This happens because he is a hired man and doesn't care about the sheep. I am the good shepherd. I know My own sheep, and they know Me, as the Father knows Me, and I know the Father. I lay down My life for the sheep. But I have other sheep that are not of this fold; I must bring them also, and they will listen to My voice. Then there will be one flock, one shepherd (John 10:11-16).

open groups). Those who best lead Sunday School departments and classes over the long haul are those persons with the gift of shepherding. Most Sunday Schools are 24/7 enterprises. Weekly Bible study, though a significant element, is only part of the Sunday School assignment. Ministry, fellowship, communication, and outreach are also best practices of growing Sunday School groups. What spiritual gift is perfectly suited for this long-term, multifaceted ministry? You guessed it: the gift of shepherding!

Read the two passages below and write down some biblical characteristics that might indicate that a person has the gift of shepherding.
John 10:11-16

_____

_____

_____

Acts 20:26-31

_____

_____

The good shepherd knows the sheep, sacrifices his life for the sheep, brings other sheep into the flock, keeps watch over the sheep, and warns the sheep of danger. Hebrews 13:20-21 calls Jesus "the great Shepherd of the sheep." Those who exercise the gift of shepherding well cause people to praise Him!

If leading a Sunday School department or class is a perfect fit for the shepherding gift, what might be good ministries in the church for those with the other grounding gifts?
Prophecy: _____
Exhortation: _____
Teaching: _____

Those with the gift of prophecy might find satisfaction on the church Christian life committee, if that committee really gives serious attention to acting on significant issues. Pro-life activities, voter-registration emphases, or world-hunger projects might also be meaningful avenues for this gift.

Most often people with this gift need a public forum to express it. That might mean a pulpit. It might mean writing. It might mean a ministry through media. It may mean vocational Christian

I testify to you this day that I am innocent of everyone's blood, for I did not shrink back from declaring to you the whole plan of God. Be on guard for yourselves and for all the flock, among whom the Holy Spirit has appointed you as overseers, to shepherd the church of God, which He purchased with His own blood. I know that after my departure savage wolves will come in among you, not sparing the flock. And men from among yourselves will rise up with deviant doctrines to lure the disciples into following them. Therefore be on the alert, remembering that night and day for three years I did not stop warning each one of you with tears (Acts 20:26-31).

May the God of peace, who brought up from the dead our Lord Jesus—the great Shepherd of the sheep—with the blood of the everlasting covenant equip you with all that is good to do His will (Heb. 13:20-21).

service! If you think God may be calling you to a preaching ministry, talk it over with your pastor.

Those with the gifts of exhortation or teaching might also find a ministry in the Sunday School. But they will need to surround themselves with others who will give attention to the areas where they differ from the shepherd. A church using a master-teacher approach, for example, will want to surround the gifted teacher with an administrator to organize the class and shepherds to lead small-group discussions and care for the group members. If your church has a Discipleship Training ministry, a women's ministry, a men's ministry, or a missions-education organization, those might be good places for the expression of teaching and exhortation. (Sometimes shepherds also make effective leaders of men's and women's groups.)

Teachers would be most effective and fulfilled in short-term seminars or classes. Exhorters make the absolute best small group leaders, including discipleship groups, support groups, recovery groups, prayer groups, etc. They can also be very effective one-on-one encouragers for new members or new Christians.

Even if God has not chosen to give you a speaking gift, perhaps you have gained understanding of these gifts and appreciation for those with those gifts. Maybe you'll even understand a little better why they speak and act the way they do!

Thank God for some of those prophets, teachers, exhorters, and shepherds who have had an impact on your spiritual growth. Print their names or initials below.

_____

_____

The Supplemental Gifts

This week you will—
- understand how the gifts of knowledge, wisdom, faith, discernment, healings, miracles, and tongues relate to the other spiritual gifts;
- understand the concept of gift mix.

Building Up the Church

Read the key verse for this week. When Paul wrote those words, he was essentially urging the troubled church at Corinth to change its focus. They were focusing on the spectacular sign gifts (tongues, miracles, healings) that edified the individuals and called attention to themselves. Paul urged them to focus on the gifts that edified the church and directed attention to Jesus. Paul encouraged them to turn their focus from themselves and toward others. They were focused too much on their own spirituality. Paul encouraged them to focus more on the spiritual health of the entire church.

The purpose of discovering and exercising your spiritual gift(s) is not just to make you a more joyful, energized, and effective believer. It certainly includes that, but it's also more. Spiritual gifts are a whole-church thing! God wants the entire church to experience congregational joy, energy, and effectiveness in being Jesus in the community where He has planted it.

Your church cannot do that unless you discover and exercise your gifts through an appropriate ministry. It cannot do that unless others—many others—in the body are also using their gifts in ministry. It cannot do that unless members and leaders have an appreciation for the gifts and ministries of others.

The main purpose of this week's study is to take a whole-church view of the spiritual gifts. We'll explore the concept of gift mix from both the individual and the church standpoint. We'll also take a brief glimpse at the supplemental gifts of faith, knowledge, wisdom, and discernment. Add those gifts to the others, mix in a healthy dose of the fruit of the Spirit, and you have the New Testament recipe for a dynamic, Christ-centered, Spirit-filled, God-honoring church!

This Week's Key Verse

Since you are eager to have spiritual gifts, try to excel in gifts that build up the church (1 Cor. 14:12).

This Week's Lessons

Day 1: The Supplemental Gifts

Day 2: The Gifts of Knowledge and Wisdom

Day 3: The Gifts of Faith and Discernment

Day 4: Macro and Micro Gifts

Day 5: Gift Mix

DAY 1

The Supplemental Gifts

We have come to the point in our study when we must deal with the controversial spiritual gifts. These gifts have been the subject of great debate and countless books. These gifts distinguish the neo-Pentecostal movement of the last century, but the controversy didn't start in the 20th century. It began in its first century. A debate over these gifts gave rise to Paul's teaching in 1 Corinthians 12–14.

Read 1 Corinthians 12:7-11 and underline the nine spiritual gifts Paul mentions.

The gifts of wisdom, knowledge, faith, healings, miracles, prophecy, distinguishing between spirits, different kinds of languages (tongues), and interpretation of languages (tongues) caused confusion in the Corinthian church and continue to receive more than their share of attention even today. Here is a brief sampling of the theological positions on this passage:

One position holds that these gifts are of a unique type called manifestations. A basic position of the neo-Pentecostal movement is that each of these gifts can be manifested in the life of every Christian. Their manifestation is a proof or sign of being Spirit filled. Others, both Pentecostal and evangelical in background, would agree about distinguishing these gifts as manifestation gifts but would argue variously that each believer (1) will manifest one and only one of these gifts, (2) definitely has one or more of these gifts, or (3) may have one or more of them.

Another position is that these gifts are of a unique type that was needed only during the founding and infancy of the church. With the completion of the New Testament, all nine of these gifts passed away, a position inferred primarily from 1 Corinthians 13:8-10.

Still another position asserts that only the sign gifts (healings, miracles, tongues, interpretation) have ceased. The gift of prophecy is also included in the out-of-commission list by some teachers. The others (wisdom, knowledge, faith, and discernment) are still evident in the church today, according to this view, although they are given a variety of definitions. Some teach that every Christian can cultivate all of the remaining gifts. Others take the "may have one or more" position.

Can you see how confusing this issue can be? This controversy has kept many folks from ever discovering one of the gifts for service we have already studied. The questions surrounding these gifts sidetrack many. In fact, this is the first chapter some folks turned to when they got this book. That's why I didn't put it first! I did not want you to get bogged down in this theological argument and miss the rich diversity of the gifts we have already covered. The gifts we have already explored in weeks 2–4 are the gifts Christ primarily uses to build His church and to accomplish His work in the world.

My position may be controversial too, but so is just about everyone else's! Here it is: If you are a Christian, God has probably entrusted you with at least one of the spiritual gifts we have already studied in weeks 2–4. If God has also granted you one or more of these gifts (tongues, interpretation, healings, miracles, wisdom, knowledge, faith, discernment), He has done so to make your team gift more effective—to supplement it.

The Sign Gifts
OK, let's deal specifically with the sign gifts: the gifts of healings, miracles, tongues, and interpretation of tongues. God has never manifested the gifts of tongues or interpretation through me. I must be honest about being skeptical about some who claim to perform miracles and healings. But I have also heard missionaries occasionally testify to supernatural occurrences involving these manifestations of the Holy Spirit, especially among people groups just being exposed to the gospel.

While struggling with this issue several years ago, I heard a veteran missionary doctor give a report that helped me. While he was visiting a Bible translator in a remote village, a woman developed severe abdominal pains. Not equipped to perform the necessary surgery, the missionary doctor simply laid his hands on her and prayed. She was healed instantly! All were amazed, even the doctor.

To deny the reality of this testimony would run the risk of blaspheming the Holy Spirit. I don't know about you, but I don't want to take that chance. As you might imagine, those in the village wanted to know more about the one in whose name the healing occurred—Jesus.

The sign gifts were evident in the infant churches of the first century. God apparently still has them at His command today to jump-start the establishment of churches among previously

The sign gifts were evident in the infant churches of the first century.

unreached peoples. (There are still literally hundreds of people groups throughout the world who have never heard the gospel in their own language.)

The danger of these sign gifts comes when they prevent a church from moving from infancy to maturity. That is the essence of Paul's exhortation to the Corinthian church. Signs point to some thing, some place, someone. It would be foolish to stop during a trip to Los Angeles to hang around a highway sign that pointed to Los Angeles. That is unfortunately what happens all too often with those who exalt the sign gifts. Their public practice is not the mark of a mature church but the mark of an immature one. What are these sign gifts?

Healings. Healings are multidimensional gifts. Yes, gifts! This word and the one for miracles are both plural in 1 Corinthians 12:9-10. It pleases God to use a person with one of the healing gifts as a partner in producing (1) physical healing, (2) emotional healing, (3) relational healing, or (4) spiritual healing in the life of another. Usually the healing involves a process that is coupled with prayer and care.

Miracles. Workers of miracles are persons whom God is pleased to use as an instrument for producing a result or solution that can only be explained supernaturally. When healing is instantaneous and takes place in a situation where human effort has been exhausted, a miracle has taken place. You only have to sit in a prayer meeting for a few minutes to understand that most Christians believe God is still in the business of healings and miracles. They may differ on whether the process is instantaneous or gradual. They may disagree about whether the touch of a human being is necessary to the process or what that process involves. But they believe God heals.

I have occasionally been confronted with this statement: "You Baptists don't believe in healing." I typically respond:

> Sure we do! Part of our cooperative missions strategy is the extension of the healing ministry of Christ. Baptists have cooperated together to establish hospitals and clinics across the country and around the world. We send short-term missionary doctors, nurses, dentists, and other medical personnel. Cooperative Program dollars support a corps of hospital chaplains who offer spiritual healing to patients and families. Baptists in many states support hospitals.

To another, faith by the same Spirit, to another, gifts of healing by the one Spirit, to another, the performing of miracles, to another, prophecy, to another, distinguishing between spirits, to another, different kinds of languages, to another, interpretation of languages (1 Cor. 12:9-10).

Once a well-known professional hockey player suffered a collapsed lung during a game against the NHL Nashville Predators. Where was he transported and treated? Baptist Hospital! Go to India or Africa, and you'll be able to find hospitals established by Baptists there too. Yes, we believe God is still in the healing business!

Tongues. The gift of tongues is the capacity a person has to speak in a language or utterance he or she has never learned. First Corinthians 12–14 was written by Paul primarily to guide the church away from an overemphasis and misuse of this gift. That material should be studied carefully. A common denominator of the gift's various uses is praise. Praise may be the universal Christian responsibility that can be associated with this gift:

> O for a thousand tongues to sing
> My great Redeemer's praise!

Interpretation of tongues. This gift is the capacity to translate the language or utterance of a message spoken in tongues.

What a powerful impact the gift of tongues had on the day of Pentecost! You can read about it in Acts 2. Pentecost was a favorite festival of the Jewish people. Jewish believers and converts had come from all over the world to camp out in Jerusalem for the festival. Because they lived in other cultures and lands, many were not fluent in the Hebrew language of their ancestors. Imagine their surprise when they heard Galileans speaking their language. It captured their attention!

The same thing happens today when missionaries enter the territory of a people with a different culture, color, or language than their own and speak to that people in their own tongue. We don't presume that God will grant our missionaries the gift of tongues. Rather, we provide them training to help them understand and communicate in the language they will need. There was no time for language school on the day of Pentecost, so God was pleased on that day to bestow this gift on the apostles.

Most of the converts eventually returned to their own countries. Where they established strong churches, it was probably because they emphasized the message of Pentecost, not the phenomenon of Pentecost. The phenomenon of tongues was not the finish line. It was the starting line. It was not the result of evangelism. It was the platform for evangelism. It was not a trophy to be envied.

The gift of tongues is the capacity a person has to speak in a language or utterance he or she has never learned.

It was a tool to be employed. These statements are true not only for tongues but for every other spiritual gift as well.

Thank God that someone spoke to you about Jesus in a language you could understand. Pray for those people around the world who have never heard the gospel in their own tongue. Pray for the missionaries who work among them. Pray for those who write music that speaks to different cultures in their language. Pray for those who live among unreached peoples and translate the Bible into their tongue. Pray for those who work to provide the film in more and more languages. Praise God for refusing to let language be a barrier to sharing the saving knowledge of Jesus Christ.

Write your prayer here. Praise God and ask for His guidance for those who use their gifts in service to Him and His church.

DAY 2

The Gifts of Knowledge and Wisdom

Jesus is the source of all knowledge and all wisdom. The gift of knowledge is more than intelligence. The gift of wisdom is way beyond common sense. These gifts are about knowing the mind of Christ.

Read Colossians 2:1-8. According to these verses, where do wisdom and knowledge come from?

_____

_____

According to 2 Peter 1:5-8 (margin, p. 88), are all Christians expected to grow in their knowledge of the faith?   ___Yes   ___No

The Gift of Knowledge

All believers are to grow in spiritual knowledge. But the spiritual gift of knowledge is a special, supplemental gift. The gift of knowledge has the capacity to understand the mind of Christ related to a subject or situation about which the Bible does not provide specific information.

Jesus sometimes exhibited an ability to read people's thoughts. He had knowledge concerning God's character and work not yet revealed in Scripture. He also had a command of the written Word and quoted it with understanding and authority. A person with the gift of knowledge usually has a supernatural capacity to recall Scripture and other information. It is the person who sometimes just knows something is wrong in your life, for example. This is the person who just knows what needs to be done in a crisis situation.

The gift of knowledge is a good partner for the gifts of administration or teaching. Among those persons who have the gifts of teaching and administration are those rare individuals whom God has also graced with the gift of knowledge. They have a unique capacity to absorb, assimilate, collate, and communicate information valuable to the work of the church.

I want you to know how great a struggle I have for you, for those in Laodicea, and for all who have not seen me in person. I want their hearts to be encouraged and joined together in love, so that they may have all the riches of assured understanding, and have the knowledge of God's mystery—Christ. In Him all the treasures of wisdom and knowledge are hidden. I am saying this so that no one will deceive you with persuasive arguments. For I may be absent in body, but I am with you in spirit, rejoicing to see your good order and the strength of your faith in Christ. Therefore as you have received Christ Jesus the Lord, walk in Him, rooted and built up in Him and established in the faith, just as you were taught, and overflowing with thankfulness. Be careful that no one takes you captive through philosophy and empty deceit based on human tradition, based on the elemental forces of the world, and not based on Christ (Col. 2:1-8).

The Gift of Wisdom

The spiritual gift of wisdom differs from the gift of knowledge in that the person so gifted has an unusual capacity to apply truth. Wisdom has the capacity to understand the mind of Christ related to the application of truth in a situation where there is not clear, specific scriptural guidance. Proverbs and parables are likely to be among the favorite parts of the Bible to a person with the gift of wisdom. Wisdom is a good companion to knowledge because it knows what to do with the information shared by the person with the gift of knowledge.

The gifts of knowledge and wisdom must be communicated to have value. In 1 Corinthians 12:8 the gifts are actually translated "a message of wisdom" and "a message of knowledge." The KJV uses "word of wisdom/word of knowledge." Though these gifts must be communicated, those who possess them are usually not quick to speak. They know what it means to pray through a situation. They typically do not speak until they are sure of God's answer. When they say, "I've prayed about this, and I think God is saying …," they really have prayed about it! Persons genuinely gifted with wisdom and knowledge, as well as discernment and faith, usually seek and expect confirmation and agreement from others with similar gifts.

Wisdom, as well as the other supplemental gifts, can be easily claimed or counterfeited by persons who don't possess them. These gifts are like spiritual dynamite, and their misuse can produce tragic results. If there is any one person in your church who has to "say the word" before anything can be done, or who can "say the word" and keep something from being done, beware. Persons with genuine spiritual gifts of wisdom, knowledge, discernment, and faith are people of the Book and people of prayer. They search the Scriptures. They search the mind of Christ. They never come to their "word of wisdom" or "word of knowledge" casually or callously. They don't pop off. When they do talk, we should listen!

If you have ever served on a pastor or staff search committee, perhaps you have been blessed by a person with a gift of wisdom. That person probably said little during the months of committee work. But while everyone was talking about praying, you knew she was really praying fervently and frequently. Those on the committee with the gift of leadership dominated most of the discussions and deliberations. A motion was made to extend an invitation for a candidate to visit the church in view of a call. But before a vote was taken, one member asked the person with the gift of wisdom,

"What is the Lord saying to you?" And her word of wisdom absolutely influenced the vote.

Wisdom and knowledge, as well as the other gifts identified in 1 Corinthians 12:7-10, including prophecy, the sign gifts (healings, miracles, tongues, interpretation of tongues), and the other supplemental gifts (wisdom, knowledge, faith, discernment) have something important in common: These gifts are superintended by the written Word of God. They are never to be a substitute for Bible study or human effort.

These gifts were exceedingly important in the early church because the Bible had not yet been completed, canonized, or circulated. We have already noted that some theologians believe that these gifts passed away when the New Testament was completed (citing 1 Cor. 13:8-10). On the other side are people who argue that every believer can cultivate every one of these gifts. This divisive debate has polarized too many Christians and too many churches.

Rather than adopting either of those polar positions, let's just agree to be consistent: Some people may have some of these gifts! All these gifts are to be measured against the Bible. Their authority never, ever supersedes the authority of Scripture. If anyone claims to have a word of wisdom or knowledge from the Lord that is clearly counter to God's written Word, do not listen to him!

Turn to the chapter in Proverbs that corresponds to today's date. Read until you find one gem of wisdom that will help you today. Then stop and record it here.

_____

_____

_____

_____

_____

Proverbs is a rich collection of words of wisdom compiled by King Solomon. There is a chapter corresponding to every day of the month. Read Psalm 111:10 and Proverbs 1:7. Would you be knowledgeable? Would you be wise? Pray. Read your Bible. Seek out those with the gifts of knowledge and wisdom. Listen to them. Learn from them. But never listen and learn from them apart from listening to and learning from the Lord and His Word.

a message of wisdom through the Spirit, to another, a message of knowledge by the same Spirit, to another, faith by the same Spirit, to another, gifts of healing by the one Spirit, to another, the performing of miracles, to another, prophecy, to another, distinguishing between spirits, to another, different kinds of languages (1 Cor. 12:7-10).

Love never ends. But as for prophecies, they will come to an end; as for languages, they will cease; as for knowledge, it will come to an end. For we know in part, and we prophesy in part. But when the perfect comes, the partial will come to an end (1 Cor. 13:8-10).

The fear of the LORD is the beginning of wisdom (Ps. 111:10).

The fear of the LORD is the beginning of knowledge (Prov. 1:7).

DAY 3
The Gifts of Faith and Discernment

All faith is a gift of God. Anyone who comes into a saving relationship with God through Jesus Christ must exercise faith.

By grace you are saved through faith, and this is not from yourselves; it is God's gift (Eph. 2:8).

To another, faith by the same Spirit (1 Cor. 12:9).

According to Ephesians 2:8, is saving faith a gift of God?
___Yes   ___No

But in 1 Corinthians 12:9 Paul is talking about an extra measure of faith beyond that needed for salvation and daily living. He is describing a spiritual gift that motivates a leader to believe the impossible and expect the improbable.

The Gift of Faith

The spiritual gift of faith is the God-given capacity to understand the mind of Christ about His future plans for a unit of the body of Christ. The person with the gift of faith sees what God's goals are when others can't see them. The person with this gift will attempt the impossible if he is convinced the idea came from God. The person with this gift exhibits extraordinary vision.

Hebrews 11 is considered the Faith Hall of Fame. Scan that chapter and write down some of the names of those mentioned:

_____

_____

All these people believed God for the impossible. That is still how the spiritual gift of faith operates today. It is more than saving faith. It is supercharged faith. The gift of faith makes an ideal partner with the gifts of leadership, prophecy, evangelism, and apostleship.

All spiritual gifts have their counterfeits. So does the gift of faith. Some people are just plain stubborn! Others are arrogant or self-serving. That is not an indicator of the gift of faith. The spiritual gift of faith is from God. Those who claim it must exercise it with great care. The key is a firm conviction that the proposed action is the will of God. It is a promise, not a wish or a dream. Faith is not a passive gift. It is active. It moves even mountains!

In any church there may be only one or two people with a gift of faith. The same is true for the gift of discernment. As one pastor told me, "You better find them!"

The Gift of Discernment

Satan is a master counterfeiter. Every spiritual gift can be counterfeited. That's one reason we need folks with the spiritual gift of discernment. Relatively speaking, few Christians are leaders. Have you ever wondered how cult leaders are able to gather so many people around them? Because most people are followers! Unchecked, they will follow those who care for them and appreciate them. This is reason enough for every church to identify those persons who have the gift of discernment.

God has given all people, lost or saved, some measure of common sense. All believers are to grow in discernment as they mature spiritually, based on their knowledge of Scripture and the indwelling of the Holy Spirit. The gift of discernment is on another level still.

The spiritual gift of discernment (or distinguishing between spirits) is the unique capacity to understand the mind of Christ concerning motives. The person with this gift is able to distinguish whether an idea, goal, teaching, action, or proposal, purported to be of God, is actually motivated by (1) God, (2) self, or (3) Satan. Like the other supplemental and sign gifts, it can also be counterfeited. The person who is consistently against the pastor probably does not have the gift. But the gift can be of extreme value when the church is making important decisions, especially if those decisions concern people and their welfare.

The gift of discernment is a particularly good partner for those with gifts of shepherding and mercy. It is a valuable ally for several other gifts as well. But shepherds and those with the gift of mercy tend to be so trusting of people that they can sometimes be blinded to the reality of situations. Those with gifts of helps and service also tend to be pushovers. All these gifts occasionally need a vote of confidence or a word of caution from a person with the gift of discernment.

Yesterday, we emphasized that spiritual gifts are not substitutes for the study of God's Word. Spiritual gifts are also no substitute for prayer. This is an important principle in the use of every spiritual gift. Prayer is even more important for those who would share a word of wisdom or a word of knowledge. Prayer is absolutely foundational, utterly indispensable, and totally inseparable from

> All believers are to grow in discernment as they mature spiritually, based on their knowledge of Scripture and the indwelling of the Holy Spirit.

It is crucial to the health of the body of Christ that anyone who says, "God wants us to do this or build that or move there or send them" is speaking a word of faith that has been received in prayer.

the exercise of the gifts of faith and discernment. It is crucial to the health of the body of Christ that anyone who says, "God wants us to do this or build that or move there or send them" is speaking a word of faith that has been received in prayer. That's obviously even more true for anyone who would speak a word of discernment. Before I would dare endorse a plan as a word from God or oppose it as a deception of Satan, I would want to be sure God had spoken. Spiritual gifts are powerful.

The New Testament word for power is *dunamis*, from which we get the English word *dynamite*. Alfred Nobel invented dynamite for constructive purposes. He established the Nobel Peace Prize in part because of his concern about being associated solely with its destructive applications. Spiritual gifts are like dynamite. Intended by God to build up individuals, churches, and cultures, their counterfeits have sometimes wrought great destruction. Handle yours with great care!

Ask God to make you a careful steward of the spiritual gift He has entrusted to you. Ask Him to help you always use your gift for good and never for harm. Thank God for those in your past whose word of faith prompted you to attempt great things for Him. Thank Him for someone whose word of discernment protected you from evil or harm.

DAY 4
Macro and Micro Gifts

Today and tomorrow I want to introduce you to three more concepts I hope will help you as you discover and employ your spiritual gifts: macro, micro, and mix. These concepts should also help you understand how and why an effective church works the way it does. Let's start off with an exercise.

In the "Team Gifts" section in the table below, circle no more than three gifts you (or others) think God may have given you. Then, in the "Supplemental Gifts" section, circle no more than one of the gifts you think might fit you. (It's OK to circle fewer than four gifts! Just don't circle more than that for the purpose of this exercise.)

TEAM GIFTS *(circle 3)*			Supplemental Gifts *(circle 1)*
Sharing Gifts	**Support Gifts**	**Speaking Gifts**	
Evangelism Apostleship	Leadership Administration	Prophecy Teaching	Faith Knowledge
Hospitality Mercy	Serving/Helps Giving	Shepherding Exhortation	Wisdom Discernment

Readers who have studied business might recognize that the terms *macro* and *micro* are basic terms in the study of economics. Macroeconomics deals with the big picture on a national or international scale. Microeconomics focuses more on the individual business unit. So the macro gifts are those that focus on the big picture in the body of Christ. The micro gifts are those whose focus is more on the individual, the small group, or a specific ministry team.

The team gifts above the heavy line in the table above are the macro gifts. Prophecy, leadership, teaching, administration, evangelism, and especially apostleship see the big picture. They share an ability to take a broad look: at the whole church, the whole community, the whole nation, or the whole world. The kingdom

> The macro gifts are those that focus on the big picture in the body of Christ. The micro gifts are those whose focus is more on the individual, the small group, or a specific ministry team.

of God is not just doctrine to them. It is an ever-present reality that guides their thinking, their planning, and their teaching. They see the local church as a vital part of a kingdom enterprise. They usually have a strong desire to see their church (or a group of churches in the case of apostleship) grow. But they also share a keen awareness concerning the growth of the kingdom of God.

You've probably heard the expression "They can't see the forest for the trees." Sometimes the opposite is true also. Those with the macro gifts sometimes can't see the trees for the forest! They have a tendency to focus so much on the big picture or on plans for the future that they sometimes lose sight of individual needs or the work of the present. That is why the micro gifts are so important and more numerous.

The micro gifts are the team gifts below the line in the table. Exhortation, helps, mercy, shepherding, service/helps, giving, and hospitality focus primarily on individual people and projects.

Which gifts are more important for the health of a church, the macro gifts or the micro gifts? Both are important! Remember the movie analogy we used earlier? The macro gifts are like the producers, directors, and major actors, whose names you see as the movie begins. The micro gifts are like the crew and the supporting cast, whose names appear only in the credits at the end of the movie. Have you ever stayed in a theater all the way to the end of the credits? How many people were left in the theater? Not many! A couple of those were probably the clean-up crew. You cannot make a good movie, or enjoy watching one, unless dozens of folks have done a good job behind the scenes for every person in the lead roles or in the manager's office.

The failure to understand this principle has perhaps caused more tension between church leaders and the people in the pews than any other single factor. Most church members would have a higher regard for their pastor, staff, and other leaders if they understood that their leaders are often motivated by the macro gifts. On the other hand, most pastors and staff leaders would probably have a greater appreciation for their members if they understood that many of them are motivated primarily by micro gifts.

Read Hebrews 13:7,17. What spiritual gifts do you think God has given your pastor? Why do you think so?

_____

_____

_____

Remember your leaders who have spoken God's word to you. As you carefully observe the outcome of their lives, imitate their faith. Obey your leaders and submit to them, for they keep watch over your souls as those who will give an account, so that they can do this with joy and not with grief, for that would be unprofitable for you (Heb. 13:7,17).

Pray for your pastor, your staff, and your church leaders. When you hear criticism of them, listen carefully to determine if that criticism has its roots in a lack of understanding about spiritual gifts. When you hear your pastor challenge the church to grow in outreach, spiritual maturity, or missions giving, remember that he is probably motivated by a strong measure of two or more macro gifts. It is a blessed church indeed where pastor and people have a healthy understanding of their spiritual gifts and appreciate how their gifts complement one another.

Shopping for Spiritual Gifts!

During our study you have completed several exercises to help you determine what spiritual gift or gifts God may have entrusted to you. Here is another of my favorites:

If I gave you a $100 gift certificate to a LifeWay Christian Store, what would you buy? What would you do with what you bought?

_____

_____

Speaking the truth in love, let us grow in every way into Him who is the head— Christ. From Him the whole body, fitted and knit together by every supporting ligament, promotes the growth of the body for building up itself in love by the proper working of each individual part (Eph. 4:15-16).

Did you ever consider that the kind of items you are attracted to in a Christian bookstore might be an indication of your spiritual gift? Look at your bookshelves. Are you attracted to books on politics, economics, tough issues like abortion or abuse, or commentaries on the end times? Maybe you have the gift of prophecy.

Or are you more likely to have books on helping people understand themselves, counseling materials, or self-help books? In the bookstore, might you gravitate to the section where self-study discipleship resources (like this one) are displayed? Might you pick up an extra copy to share with someone else? Maybe you have the gift of exhortation.

Perhaps you head to the tract rack to see what's new in witnessing resources. Or maybe you scour the shelves of books on apologetics, hoping to find the perfect book for your friend at work who has been "educated past religion" or another who is caught up in the New Age movement or being deceived by a cult. If so, maybe God has entrusted you with the gift of evangelism.

Maybe you shy away from the books altogether and head to the gift section to buy something special for a new parent, a new member, or a new neighbor. Or maybe just something pretty for the class fellowship at your home next Friday? Perhaps God has given you the gift of hospitality.

One of the key character-
istics of a teacher is that
he loves charts, maps,
graphs, and lists.

If you are one of those people who might spend hours in the bookstore, choosing carefully how to get the most for your $100, you might just have the gift of teaching! One of the key characteristics of a teacher is that he loves charts, maps, graphs, and lists. (So do those with the gift of administration.) It would not be unusual for a person with the gift of teaching to buy an entire book just to get one really great chart or graph. He or she might buy a book on the sale table just because the table of contents outlines the subject in an orderly fashion. (OK, I confess: that's a personal testimony!)

Maybe you resent the fact that I am making you spend the $100 on yourself at all! You would rather give the $100 to missions or use it to buy canned goods for your church's food pantry ministry. Maybe God has blessed you with the gift of giving or the gift of mercy.

Perhaps you found yourself having mixed feelings about how you'd use the $100. You might spend $50 one way, $30 another, and $20 still another way. That might be a clue that you have a mix of spiritual gifts. We'll explore that concept tomorrow.

DAY 5
Gift Mix

Some individuals have a mix of spiritual gifts. Every church has a mix of spiritual gifts. Every ministry within a church needs a mix of spiritual gifts. The saying "Birds of a feather flock together" is certainly true of spiritual gifts. Some folks even suggest that churches should attempt to form ministries around certain spiritual gifts. Get all those with the gift of mercy together for the benevolence team. Gather all the evangelists together for the outreach team. You get the idea.

Be careful about taking this approach! Virtually every ministry in the church needs a mixture of gifts to be effective. God may even have equipped you with a mixture of gifts just right for a particular kind of ministry. Some gifts also have common characteristics.

Evangelism, Leadership, and Prophecy
Persons with the gifts of evangelism, leadership, and prophecy share some similar characteristics:
- Known as having strong, confident, often dominant personalities.
- Sometimes considered pushy by others.
- Don't like to take no for an answer.
- Don't mind being the center of attention.
- Believe what they have to say is both true and important.
- Prefer to get things started and turn the follow-up or follow-through over to someone else.
- Tend to be impatient. Really have to depend on the Holy Spirit for patience.
- The word *impossible* is not a part of their vocabulary. Will tackle the tough situations.

Administration, Teaching, and Apostleship
Those with the gifts of administration, teaching, and often apostleship also share some common characteristics:
- Have strong, confident, often dominant personalities but not to the same degree as those with gifts of prophecy and leadership.
- Are comfortable in a subordinate role to a gifted leader.

Every church has a mix of spiritual gifts.

- Say amen to 1 Corinthians 14:40: "Everything must be done decently and in order."
- Prefer a clear presentation of the facts.
- Appreciate the value of policies, procedures, and guidelines (especially if they prepared them).
- Advocate a team approach to ministry. Like committee work more than they admit!

We have already noted how the micro gifts are more concerned with individuals than the macro gifts. Whereas the macro gifts prefer a crowd, those with the gifts of hospitality, service, and shepherding are more comfortable working with small groups. Those with the gifts of mercy, helps, and exhortation can also work with smaller groups, but they are just as comfortable working one on one.

The gift of service makes sure everything is ready for people to have a pleasant experience. The gift of hospitality draws people into the fellowship. The gift of shepherding helps them connect and goes searching for them if they wander away! For the most part those with any of these three gifts are eager to serve. They just prefer to be asked. Some people may respond to the appeal for volunteers from the pulpit or in the newsletter. But most will not. Does that mean they don't want to serve? No. It just means they want to be asked!

Those with micro gifts don't require a lot of attention. They don't serve for public affirmation. All they want to know is that their leaders know what they do and appreciate their efforts. Just a little pat on the back from the leaders and administrators who enlisted them is usually all it takes to keep them going.

From Ephesians 4:12 we learn that one of the main purposes of spiritual gifts is to equip God's people. The word translated *training* has a double meaning. It can mean *to prepare*. And it can also mean *to repair*. The Greeks used it as a medical term to describe setting a broken bone.

Read Galatians 6:1-5. The word translated *restore* is the same word that can be translated *equip*. There was another reason for having you read these verses. Did this passage resonate deep within you? Do you have a strong inner desire to help people get back on their feet? Do you like to root for the underdog? Are you thrilled to hear comeback stories? Those characteristics are common to those with the gifts of exhortation, helps, and mercy.

... for the training of the saints in the work of ministry, to build up the body of Christ (Eph. 4:12).

Brothers, if someone is caught in any wrongdoing, you who are spiritual should restore such a person with a gentle spirit, watching out for yourselves so you won't be tempted also. Carry one another's burdens; in this way you will fulfill the law of Christ. For if anyone considers himself to be something when he is nothing, he is deceiving himself. But each person should examine his own work, and then he will have a reason for boasting in himself alone, and not in respect to someone else. For each person will have to carry his own load (Gal. 6:1-5).

The double meaning of the word *equip* is perhaps best seen in Matthew 4:21. Circle the word.

Going on from there, He saw two other brothers, James the son of Zebedee, and his brother John. They were in a boat with Zebedee their father, mending their nets, and He called them (Matt. 4:21).

Just before Jesus called James and John to join Him in fishing for men, they were "mending" their nets. The NIV uses "preparing." What was the purpose of these repairs? To make the nets useful again! So they were preparing the nets by repairing them. Sometimes even God's people need to have some repair work done before they can be effectively used in ministry. That is the specialty of those with the gifts of mercy, helps, and exhortation. You will remember that *exhortation* literally means *to come alongside to help*. In a sense that is true for all three of these gifts. Aren't you glad God has placed gifted people like this in your church?

One time someone who thought he had discovered a system emerging from the discussion above observed, "I'll bet no one has the gifts of both prophecy and mercy. They are almost totally opposite from each other." That is probably generally true. In reality, however, I know several people who exhibit both gifts. They form the core of most successful crisis-pregnancy ministries. The prophet in them hates abortion. The gift of mercy in them loves the young women who think that abortion is their only alternative. The prophet in them certainly tries to communicate to a woman the horrors of ending the beautiful life that has begun within her. The mercy gift in them wants to make sure the woman has the support necessary to make a decision for life.

In terms of gift mix, crisis pregnancy centers also need administrators, servants, helpers, exhorters, and evangelists. A woman with the gift of hospitality would be a great receptionist too, to put a frightened young woman or couple at ease. This is just one example of how several spiritual gifts can enhance a ministry, even if that ministry has a core of folks motivated by a particular gift mix. It's all about teamwork. It's about helping people know Jesus clearly and completely. And doing it with love—together!

Individual believers may have a wide mix of gifts. Let me use my own gift mix as an example. My primary gift mix is leadership, teaching, and exhortation. Two of these are macro gifts. The other one is a micro gift. The gift of exhortation provides an element of people person to how God made me. That helps (sometimes!) to temper the domineering characteristics associated with the leadership gift. I also usually score high on the gifts of knowledge and discernment on spiritual gifts inventories. I am currently trying to understand how God wants me to use those gifts to supplement my mix.

One way I will do that is by seeking confirmation and counsel from others. You see, it is often easier to see another's gifts than your own! So ask someone you trust to help you evaluate the gift mix God has entrusted to you.

Perhaps you have been struggling to figure out which of the gifts is your primary gift. Relax! Maybe God has given you a strong measure of two or three gifts. This is your gift mix. Your goal will be to involve yourself in a ministry that fits your mix of gifts.

WEEK 6

Putting It All Together

This week you will—
- review the basic principles about spiritual gifts;
- review the gifts and explore possible ways to use them;
- understand the difference between spiritual gifts and the corresponding responsibilities of all believers;
- understand that the gifts of the Spirit must be exercised in tandem with the fruit of the Spirit.

Time to Nail It All Down!

You've almost made it! Even if you are not yet certain about what spiritual gift(s) God has given to you, I hope you have a few hints. And I hope you have a deeper appreciation of God's design for the church. He has gifted every church with the mix of spiritual gifts needed to accomplish His purposes for that congregation.

I once heard churches described as public-relations firms for Jesus. For people to see your church as a complete picture of the love, forgiveness, compassion, comfort, direction, and power available through Jesus Christ, each member of your church must be mobilized for ministry. Those various ministries will be most effective if the folks involved are motivated by their spiritual gifts.

Such churches are joyous places to work and worship. When each member is doing his or her part, and trusting other members to do their parts, there's no time for criticism. Each member appreciates the gifts of leaders. Leaders appreciate the gifts of the members. Leaders affirm the gifts of the other leaders. Members affirm the gifts of the other members. Everyone works together. The result is a magnetic church. Jesus is lifted up. People are drawn to Jesus. The church is blessed. People are saved. They grow in Christlikeness. God is honored.

No church is perfect. I have never heard of a church where all members use their spiritual gifts. As a church leader, my dream is that every active member of our church could answer the question, What is your ministry? The answer would indicate that they are using their spiritual gift or in the process of discovering it. This is probably an idealistic goal, but isn't it one worthy of pursuit? Will you enlist in the cause?

This Week's Key Verse

Just as each of us has one body with many members, and these members do not all have the same function, so in Christ we who are many form one body, and each member belongs to all the others (Rom. 12:4-5).

This Week's Lessons

Day 1: Let's Review!
Day 2: The Along-the-Way and Out-of-the-Way Principle
Day 3: Gifts and Kingdom Economics
Day 4: Putting the Gifts to Work
Day 5: Gifts and Fruit

DAY 1
Let's Review!

In the first week of our study, we explored some basic principles about spiritual gifts: When Jesus of Nazareth walked this earth, He fully possessed and exercised every spiritual gift. When He returned to heaven, He distributed those gifts through the Holy Spirit. Like the gift of salvation, these gifts are free. You need only acknowledge and receive them. Each believer has been given at least one spiritual gift. Some have two or more. Some have a stronger measure of a gift than another person with that same gift. That is God's sovereign choice. He chooses the gift. We are simply to receive our gifts gladly, unwrap them, and put them to use in ministry. When we do, God is honored, and the church is built up.

We defined a spiritual gift as a God-given assignment, capacity, and desire to perform a function within the body of Christ with supernatural joy, energy, and effectiveness. God chooses our gifts to be compatible with, but not identical to, our natural talents, our personalities, our experiences, our passions, and the skills we have learned. According to Psalm 139:14-15, He programmed us just the way He wanted us to be.

God allows us to choose to "run the program" or to reject it. Discovering our spiritual gifts is an important part of understanding God's will for our lives.

I will praise You
  because I am unique
  in remarkable ways.
Your works are wonderful,
  and I know this very well.
My bones were not hidden
  from You
  when I was made in secret,
when I was formed in the
  depths of the earth
  (Ps. 139:14-15).

Using just the first letter as a clue, see if you can complete each of the spaces below with the name of the spiritual gift.

Support Gifts	Sharing Gifts	Speaking Gifts	Supplemental Gifts
Service/H ————	H ————————	S ————————	W ————————
G ————————	M ————————	E ————————	D ————————
A ————————	A ————————	T ————————	K ————————
L ————————	E ————————	P ————————	F ————————

See how it all fits together! Imagine what an awesome, magnetic fellowship your church would be if there were actually names of people in each of those boxes! You would expect there to be more names in some boxes than others if the church has a healthy balance and mix of gifts.

As you discover your gift, or help others to discover their gifts, don't worry too much about figuring out what specific gift God has given you before you start doing something. Start with the big categories. Do you think your primary gift is probably a macro gift or a micro gift? Or put another way, do you see forests or trees? After you have determined that, decide whether you think your primary gift is a speaking gift, a support gift, or a sharing gift. Do any of the supplemental gifts give you additional hints about your primary gift?

The idea is to zero in on your gift as closely as you can. Then experiment! Take on a ministry responsibility in your church where that gift would add value. Work hard. Get training to develop your gift. Read books. Attend conferences. Observe other people who exhibit that gift. Stick with it for a while. Honor whatever commitment of time you have made. (If that is not clear, negotiate a time limit. Six months to a year ought to be long enough.)

Then evaluate. Are you experiencing joy? Is God providing the energy for the job, giving you extra physical, emotional, and spiritual strength while you are involved in ministry? Are you being effective? Do others say things to affirm your own evaluation? If the answers are yes, then you have probably discovered one of your spiritual gifts.

If not, try again. Maybe your gift is in the adjacent column on the chart, or its the one above or below it. Go through the process again.

When you discover a gift, are you finished? Maybe. Maybe not. Some people have been given more than one spiritual gift—a gift mix. I have a theory, confirmed unscientifically by years of personal observation, that most pastors and other vocational ministers often have a gift mix of two, three, or all four of the gifts in one of the four rows (not columns) on the chart on the previous page (for example, prophecy-leader, teacher-administrator, or shepherding-hospitality). Would your pastor fit on one of those rows?

If my theory is true of your pastor and other church leaders, does that help you understand them better? If God made them

Micro Gifts
- Service/Helps
- Giving
- Hospitality
- Mercy
- Shepherding
- Exhortation
- Wisdom
- Discernment

Macro Gifts
- Prophecy
- Teaching
- Leadership
- Administration
- Evangelism
- Apostleship
- Faith
- Knowledge

Brothers, we ask and encourage you in the Lord Jesus, that as you have received from us how you must walk and please God—as you are doing—do so even more. ... to seek to lead a quiet life, to mind your own business, and to work with your own hands, as we commanded you, so that you may walk properly in the presence of outsiders and not be dependent on anyone (1 Thess. 4:1,11-12).

that way and called them to lead your church, what might that indicate about God's plan for your church? How do your own gifts complement those of your pastor and leaders? If you are a leader, how might your gifts be misunderstood by those who are motivated by other gifts?

I think Paul's reason for writing to the Corinthian church, the Roman church, and the Ephesian church about spiritual gifts was not primarily to get the hearers to take a job in the church—or even to discover their spiritual gifts. Developing a full-employment church is certainly implied, but it is not the main thing. What God was trying to say to these early churches through Paul is the same message many churches need to hear today: "Get along!" A healthy understanding of the doctrine of spiritual gifts among both leaders and members will help a church build a foundation for harmony and life-changing ministry.

When Paul wrote to the Thessalonian church, it had become sort of a lazy church. At least some of its members had become lazy. Meditate on 1 Thessalonians 4:1,11-12 and ask God to help you become all He wants you to be. Write your prayer below.

DAY 2

The Along-the-Way and Out-of-the-Way Principle

Your spiritual gift or gift mix helps you determine the priorities for ministry God expects of you. But your gift is not a blanket excuse to avoid universal Christian responsibilities. This is one of the most confusing things about spiritual gifts. On the one hand, the Bible teaches that only Jesus has every spiritual gift. Therefore, no one of us can ever think, feel, or act just like Jesus. On the other hand, the Bible also teaches that we are to grow toward Christlikeness. Therefore, we should desire and strive to be as much like Jesus as humanly possible.

This paradox is made even more complicated by the fact that some Bible commandments for all believers seem to parallel a spiritual gift. The one-another passages are one example of this paradox.

Circle the words in the passages to the right that are the same as or similar to words we have associated with spiritual gifts.

How do we deal with this paradox?

Some suggest that the only way to do so is to insist that every believer should cultivate every spiritual gift. That would certainly be a noble ambition. If attained, it could result in Christlikeness. But the Bible clearly teaches that every Christian does not have every spiritual gift. So we must reject that lofty aspiration.

On day 4 of week 1, we discovered that the command in 1 Corinthians 12:31, "Desire the greater gifts," was directed toward the church as a whole, not to individuals. The verb translated "desire" is plural in the Greek. In English translations it is often impossible to distinguish whether a command is directed toward *you* singular or *you* plural. A Texas Bible translation could distinguish the latter with *y'all!*

What's the point? Simply that many of the commands in Scripture that we tend to apply to individuals are actually directed toward the church as a whole. The commands are not "Each and every one of you show hospitality (or confess your

You are called to freedom, brothers; only don't use this freedom as an opportunity for the flesh, but serve one another through love (Gal. 5:13).

Share with the saints in their needs; pursue hospitality (Rom. 12:13).

Give back to Caesar the things that are Caesar's, and to God the things that are God's (Matt. 22:21).

Let the message about the Messiah dwell richly among you, teaching and admonishing one another in all wisdom, and singing psalms, hymns, and spiritual songs, with gratitude in your hearts to God (Col. 3:16).

Encourage each other daily, while it is still called today, so that none of you is hardened by sin's deception (Heb. 4:13).

Get wisdom, get understanding (Prov. 4:5).

Grow in the grace and knowledge of our Lord and Savior Jesus Christ (2 Pet. 3:18).

sins!) to each and every one of you." It is a corporate command. The command is to the church. This position is compatible with the doctrine of spiritual gifts. In fact, the appropriate use of spiritual gifts is the only way to accomplish these collective commands!

Many have suggested that an appropriate translation of the Great Commission (Matt. 28:18-20) would be "As you go, make disciples." This is where we get the as-you-go principle. You should be ready to minister in the name of Christ as you go, even if the situation would be better served by a person with a more appropriate gift. Your spiritual gifts, on the other hand, motivate and equip you to go out of your way to exercise them. Your gifts help you determine the ministries in which you will intentionally engage, make an extra effort to do, and give priority time to preparation and training. As you mature in Christ and realize the areas in which you are not gifted, you will want to develop some skills in those other areas to help you when you encounter an along-the-way situation at home, at school, or at work. Who will you want to provide such training? Of course, a person who has a spiritual gift in that area!

This topic is perhaps the most overlooked subject in writings about spiritual gifts. It is often avoided altogether because of the possibility for confusion. I hope this discussion has not confused you but has helped you. The table which follows may add extra clarification.

In the table below, add your ideas to the kinds of activities that would fit in the along-the-way and out-of-the-way columns corresponding to each spiritual gift. Remember that the along-the-way items should relate to all Christians. The activities in the out-of-the-way column should be only those someone with that spiritual gift might do.

Spiritual Gift	Along the Way (Any Believer)	Out of the Way (Those with the Gift)
Faith	Believe God's promises during personal or family illness or crisis.	Pursue a vision from the Lord in the face of serious obstacles or opposition.
Knowledge	Read the Bible. Attend Sunday School.	Carefully study the Bible. Memorize much of it.

Spiritual Gift	Along the Way (Any Believer)	Out of the Way (Those with the Gift)
Wisdom	Study and apply the Book of Proverbs.	Spend much time with God in prayer seeking His answer to a complex issue.
Discernment	Don't believe everything you hear on television (even from TV preachers!)	Through deep prayer, receive an insight you know to be from God about a person, message, or issue.
Prophecy	Stay informed about public-policy issues and vote with a Christian perspective.	Speak out boldly about issues that affect God's people.
Teaching	Explain Bible stories to your children.	Carefully construct lessons that cause people to learn and apply Bible truths.
Shepherding	Guard, protect, and provide for the needs of your household. Be an example.	Take a long-term responsibility for a Sunday School class or small group.
Exhortation	Encourage your children and discipline them when necessary.	Be the facilitator for a discipleship group or an encourager for a new Christian.
Leadership	Exert spiritual leadership in your home. Lead your family in prayer and church attendance.	Attempt significant projects for the advancement of the kingdom of God.
Administration	Manage your resources and those in your household well.	Serve on the finance, personnel, or building committees. Lead a fund-raising campaign.

Spiritual Gift	Along the Way (Any Believer)	Out of the Way (Those with the Gift)
Serving	Do your part of the household chores. Help out around the church.	Participate in workdays at the church. Set up chairs for Sunday School. Serve on the sound team, in the library, as an usher.
Helps	Make coffee or pass out materials for your Sunday School department director.	Volunteer in the church office. Help straighten out the music library. Pay a staff member's way to a conference.
Evangelism	Participate in evangelism training. Witness to persons as you have opportunity.	Be an equipper in the evangelism training ministry. Be active in church visitation. Serve as a Sunday School outreach leader. Join the decision counseling team.
Giving	Tithe. Give special offerings to missions and other causes as God leads.	Give regularly beyond a tithe. Contribute generously to special projects and people.
Hospitality	Sign up for a turn to bring doughnuts to Sunday School.	Serve as the fellowship leader in your Sunday School department or class.
Mercy	Mow the lawn of the widow down the street. Then drink the glass of lemonade she offers!	Volunteer at the homeless shelter, the soup kitchen, or some other ministry.
Apostleship	Go on a mission trip. Volunteer for a short-term missions assignment.	Volunteer for missionary service through the International Mission Board, the North American Mission Board, or another agency.

DAY 3
Gifts and Kingdom Economics

I am fascinated by economics. For example, I'm amazed that the opening of a new business in a community with just a few dozen new jobs can have an economic impact many times larger than the combined salaries of the new employees. There is a multiplying effect when new money is introduced into a community's economy. More people shop at the grocery store, so a new clerk is added. The department store's sales increase. More people eat at the restaurant. The restaurant owner builds an addition to the building, using products made by the new business, and adds employees. This cycle goes on in multiple directions at the same time. The economic pie is being cut into more pieces, but the pie is bigger, so the slices are still at least as big as they used to be!

In God's kingdom economy a similar multiplying effect occurs when spiritual gifts are put to work in God-honoring ministries. In 1 Corinthians 12:4-6 Paul wrote about the relationship of gifts, ministries, and activities. The following story will help illustrate the concept.

I do not have the gift of mercy. As an associate pastor, I had frequent opportunities to visit people in the hospital and to deal with families who had experienced the death of a loved one. A person with the gift of mercy is excellent in these situations. I have the gift of exhortation. I discovered that to have a positive effect in those situations, I had to operate in that gift. It worked! Not only did I stop dreading such situations, but I actually felt joy, confidence, and effectiveness through the gift of exhortation.

I recall a night that illustrates this. Late one evening I received a call that Gus was dying. I knew that his wife, Dot, and daughter, Nancy, needed a word of encouragement. When I arrived in the hospital room, they had stepped out, so I took out a calling card, wrote the words "Fear not" on it, and tacked it to a small bulletin board in the room. When Dot and Nancy returned to retrieve their belongings, they saw those words of encouragement just when they needed them. I repeated those words at the memorial service, then again for several months whenever I saw them. The effect of comfort was the same as the gift of mercy but was expressed through the gift of exhortation.

There are different gifts, but the same Spirit. There are different ministries, but the same Lord. And there are different activities, but the same God is active in everyone and everything (1 Cor. 12:4-6).

Another example comes from the hospitality team at First Baptist Church of Garland, Texas. Women who did not have the gift of evangelism faithfully went out each Thursday morning to visit newcomers to the community. They had the gift of hospitality. They were armed with a beautiful basket or bag filled with information about the church and community and a loaf of fresh bread prepared by a team of women with gifts of service and helps. These women often have opportunities to share a word about the Lord. Some of the newcomers attend the church—not because people with gifts of evangelism came but through the gifts of hospitality and service.

Consider the multiplying effect on a first-time visitor to a church where the people are using their gifts. The visitors are greeted by a member of the parking lot team with the gift of service and directed to the right door. A greeter with the gift of hospitality points them to the welcome center, where other similarly gifted folks escort each family member to his or her class. Again greeters meet them there and make them feel welcome. They meet a few folks, then sit down in the chairs that were arranged on Saturday by people with the gift of service.

After the group sings a chorus led by an exhorter who loves music, the department director takes over. He is obviously a gifted leader. Our guests move to a class where six or eight couples enjoy a relevant study of the Bible led by a teacher with the gift of shepherding. Another with the gift of hospitality or exhortation accompanies our guests to the worship center and helps the visitors find a place. They gaze at the bulletin, prepared earlier in the week by a person with the gift of helps. The choir, made up of folks with a variety of gifts, leads the congregation into worship. The pastor, equipped with a strong gift of prophecy, preaches a powerful message.

The next week, an outreach team from the Sunday School class, which includes one member with the gift of evangelism and a couple of others who are learning to witness more effectively, visits in their home. After a presentation of the gospel, our Sunday guests ask Jesus to save them. The next Sunday, in the decision counseling area, they meet a new member encourager, one with the gift of exhortation, who will guide them through a study of *Survival Kit* or another foundational study. That afternoon they attend a new member seminar led by a gifted teacher. Later they are introduced to the doctrine of spiritual gifts, discover theirs, and begin a ministry of their

Consider the multiplying effect on a first-time visitor to a church where the people are using their gifts.

own. And the cycle continues. That's the kind of powerful effect a church can have when members are mobilized for ministry around their spiritual gifts.

One of the most powerful effects of spiritual gifts operating throughout the life of a church's economy is the multiplying effect among believers. Discouraged evangelists need exhorters to come beside them and pump them up. Prophets who are worried about paying the bills can't concentrate on the Word and prayer; they need sensitive givers to come to the rescue. Sunday School teachers, the champions of shepherding, sometimes get sick. They need the ministry of someone with the gift of mercy. Those with the gift of helps sometimes need someone to pitch in and help them, too! I've smiled secretly hundreds of times when I have seen one church secretary help another with a last-minute request from a staff member. One helper helping another, both expressing the gift of helps!

A manifestation of the Spirit is given to each person to produce what is beneficial (1 Cor. 12:7).

On the chart below, circle the number beside each gift that indicates whether you primarily give or receive the spiritual benefits of that gift. Unless you have a lot of gifts, you should have more low numbers than high ones!

I Receive the Benefits						I Provide the Benefits				
Prophecy	1	2	3	4	5	6	7	8	9	10
Teaching	1	2	3	4	5	6	7	8	9	10
Shepherding	1	2	3	4	5	6	7	8	9	10
Exhortation	1	2	3	4	5	6	7	8	9	10
Leadership	1	2	3	4	5	6	7	8	9	10
Administration	1	2	3	4	5	6	7	8	9	10
Serving/Helps	1	2	3	4	5	6	7	8	9	10
Evangelism	1	2	3	4	5	6	7	8	9	10
Giving	1	2	3	4	5	6	7	8	9	10
Hospitality	1	2	3	4	5	6	7	8	9	10
Mercy	1	2	3	4	5	6	7	8	9	10
Apostleship	1	2	3	4	5	6	7	8	9	10

Which three gifts have the highest numbers?

_____ _____ _____

Does this give you any further indication of the gift(s) God may have given you?

Putting the Gifts to Work

Spiritual gifts
Experiences
Relational style
Vocational skills
Enthusiasm

Spiritual gifts
Heart
Abilities
Personality
Experiences

By grace you are saved through faith, and this is not from yourselves; it is God's gift—not from works, so that no one can boast. For we are His creation—created in Christ Jesus for good works, which God prepared ahead of time so that we should walk in them (Eph. 2:8-10).

Personality discovery
Learning spiritual gifts
Abilities awareness
Connecting passion to ministry
Experiences of life

It is finally time to consider some of the ministry possibilities for discovering or exercising your spiritual gift. In God's kingdom economy your spiritual gift is the primary factor in determining your ministry, but it is not the only one. God has entrusted you with the stewardship of at least one spiritual gift. He also expects you to be a good steward of the other aspects of who you are—your passions, personality, temperament, relational style, life experiences, financial resources, station in life, influence, intellect, citizenship, and any number of other factors. You should take advantage of any opportunity you have to know yourself.

Discovering your spiritual gift is a key step in knowing yourself spiritually. (For help in identifying the other factors that influence meaningful ministry, see the SERVE model in *Jesus on Leadership* by Gene Wilkes.[1] Your church can use a similar approach to help members find a good ministry fit, using various other acronyms like Rick Warren's SHAPE[2] or Jay McSwain's PLACE.[3])

Ephesians 2:8-9 is often quoted to emphasize that a person can only come to Christ by grace through faith. In verse 10 Paul wrote the why of verses 8-9. Read all three verses together.

According to these verses, God did not just save us for heaven. For what purpose did He create us?

_____

_____

God created us to do good works. Our purpose in life is to minister. Putting our spiritual gifts to work in ministry is the best way to do the kind of good works that honor God and express our thankfulness to Him for the free gift of salvation through Jesus Christ.

The following chart has some ideas for matching your spiritual gift with a ministry. These are only suggestions. Each church is organized differently. Some have teams; other have committees; still others have both. Some have Sunday Schools; others have weekday home

or cell groups for Bible study. Some have women's ministries; some have men's ministries; others have both; some have neither!

The suggestions are just thought starters. Your assignment is to think of at least one other ministry in your church that might use the corresponding gift. If your church doesn't have the position mentioned, cross it out. If your church has a program or position that is similar, correct the chart. Or color outside the lines and think of a brand new ministry! (That's how most of the ministries on the chart got started in the first place—by someone who had a gift, a passion, a dream, or a burden and responded from giftedness.) If you are studying this material with a group, share your ideas to get a more complete list.

Gift	Some Ministries Where You Might Discover Joy, Energy, and Effectiveness
Prophecy	Preaching (church, nursing home, jail), Christian-life committee
Teaching	Discipleship seminars, leadership training, new-member-orientation classes, tutoring, literacy, Vacation Bible School, Children's Choir director, missions-organization leader
Shepherding	Sunday School teacher or department director, Vacation Bible School director or teacher, Sunday School care-group leader, small-group leader
Exhortation	Discipleship group leader, facilitator for a support group, new-Christian encourager team, lay-counseling ministry, English as a second language, tutoring, missions-organization leader, recreation-ministry leader, Upward Basketball[4] coach, youth camp sponsor/counselor
Leadership	Director or chairman of any church program, ministry, committee, team, or department; strategic (or long-range) planning committee or task force
Administration	Director or coordinator of or any ministry, team, or department. Member of committees like finance, personnel, properties
Serving	Sunday School care-group leader, ushers team, Vacation Bible School crossing guards, sound-and-lighting team, audiovisual team, setup team, landscaping team, properties team, parking team, transportation team, church-library team, banner ministry, food-service team, Lord's Supper preparation

	team, baptism team, music-ministry librarian, choir robe captain or section leader, children's choir helper, missions-organization counselor
Helps	Church office work, Sunday School department or class secretary, anything with *assistant* in the title of the position, quietly meeting the needs of the pastor, staff member, or their family
Evangelism	Outreach/evangelism leader in a Sunday School class or department, equipper/trainer in an evangelism-training program or strategy, decision counselors for worship services/revivals/crusades (*DecisionTime*[5] is an excellent training resource.)
Giving	Giving to regular budgeted church ministries; giving to special missions offerings for international missions, North American missions, World Hunger Fund; giving to building programs; love offerings to special guests; special offerings for persons in need; extras for pastor and staff members; perhaps serving on finance committee or personnel committee
Hospitality	Parking-lot team, greeters team, guest/information center, Sunday School department/class greeter, hospitality-ministry team, Sunday School department/class fellowship leader; newcomer team
Mercy	Hospital-visitation team, nursing-home team, homebound ministry, grief-support ministry, food pantry, clothes closet, other benevolent ministries, crisis-pregnancy ministry
Apostleship	Organizing mission trips, educating and informing others about missions, volunteering for missionary appointment

1. Gene Wilkes, *Jesus on Leadership* (Nashville: LifeWay Press, 1996).
2. Rick Warren, *The Purpose-Driven Church* (Grand Rapids, MI: Zondervan, 1995); Rick Warren, *The Purpose-Driven Life* (Grand Rapids, MI: Zondervan, 2002).
3. Place Ministries, *www.placeministries.org*.
4. Upward Basketball, *www.upward.com*.
5. Yvonne Burrage, *DecisionTime* (Nashville: LifeWay Press, 1998).

DAY 5
Gifts and Fruit

First Corinthians 13, the Bible's great love chapter, is right in the middle of Paul's major teaching on spiritual gifts. The teaching of the chapter can be summarized like this: Spiritual gifts, however spectacular, exercised without love, have no effect. They are nothing—nada, zilch, zero. Some people suggest a devotional plan where the reader supplements whatever else is being studied by alternating every other day between 1 Corinthians 13 (the love chapter) and Hebrews 11 (the faith chapter). It's not a bad plan, at least for a period of time.

It would certainly not be a bad idea for someone who is beginning to discover and use his or her spiritual gift(s). The biggest threat to the effective use of spiritual gifts is pride. That was the basic problem in the church in Corinth. Not unlike young children, you can almost hear some of the Corinthians chanting, "My gift's better than your gift." No gift is better than another. If one person is more effective than another person with the same gift, it could mean one of them needs more training. Or it could just mean God decided that the one person could handle a larger measure of that gift. Either way there is no place for pride or envy when it comes to spiritual gifts.

The gifts of the Spirit must always be exercised in concert with the fruit of the Spirit. Paul described the fruit of a Spirit-controlled life in Galatians 5:22-23.

There was little or no punctuation in the original Greek manuscripts of the New Testament. Some scholars suggest that there should be a colon after the word love, thus making the verse read, "The fruit of the Spirit is love: ..." That would be compatible with Paul's elevation of love in 1 Corinthians 13.

Spiritual gifts must be exercised in the context of love. But the reverse is true also. The fruit of the Spirit in the life of a person, by themselves, don't make much difference in the world. Being a good person without producing any good works doesn't really accomplish God's purposes. In fact, a person who takes this to an extreme is akin to a monk. I guess that's better than the person who exercises spiritual gifts without the fruit of the spirit. That person sometimes can act like a spiritual monster. You have probably known some. I have too. God doesn't

The fruit of the Spirit is love, joy, peace, patience, kindness, goodness, faith [or faithfulness], gentleness, self-control. Against such things there is no law (Gal. 5:22-23).

want us to be monks or monsters. He wants us to exercise spiritual gifts and demonstrate spiritual fruit all at the same time.

This is the last exercise in our study. Complete it prayerfully. Beside each of the fruit in the chart below are a few ideas about how that fruit affects the way you should discover and use your spiritual gift(s). Add your own thoughts in the margin. May God bless you as you exercise the gifts and fruit of His Spirit.

Fruit of the Spirit	How This Fruit Relates to Spiritual Gifts
Love	The only proper motive for discovering your spiritual gifts is the Great Commandment: an honest desire to love God with all your heart, soul, mind, and strength, and to love your neighbor as yourself. Jesus exercised all the spiritual gifts and did so consistently in love.
Joy	Joy is deeper than two emotions sometimes confused with it, pleasure and happiness. Your spiritual gift may not always bring you pleasure, and in fact, it may lead to hard work. It will almost certainly lead you to minister in some situations that are not happy. But you can count on it helping you experience a joy like no other—the joy of knowing you are being used as a channel of blessing from God Himself.
Peace	There is no other peace like the inner peace of knowing you are in the will of God. Discovering and using your spiritual gift is an important part of understanding God's good, pleasing, and perfect will for your life.
Patience	It may take time to discover your primary spiritual gift. You could discover that God has given you a number of gifts, a gift mix. Don't worry, though. As long as you are on the journey, God will be patient with you. Also realize that you will be developing your gift for a lifetime. You will never fully arrive. Have you ever noticed that doctors and lawyers operate a practice, not a perfect? Your gift will never be perfectly and completely developed. This fruit of the spirit will be particularly important to you if you discover God has given you the gift of leadership, prophecy, evangelism, or mercy. Your tendency is to be impatient. You will need to trust in the Lord's timing. Don't let the lack of patience destroy relationships with the very people who need the positive impact of your gift.

Kindness   A lack of kindness can also destroy the otherwise positive impact of your spiritual gift. You will want to pay special attention to cultivating this fruit if you discover that God has given you the gift of administration, teaching, or giving. Because these gifts are so organized and deliberate, they have a tendency to be abrupt. Those with these gifts would say they are just matter of fact; others might call them rude! This is often said about those with the gifts of prophecy and leadership as well. Be kind!

Goodness   This word could be translated *Godness*. That's what goodness is. When you exercise your spiritual gift, people should praise God. They may thank you too, and that's OK. But ultimately the good works you do should point people to Jesus. That, after all, is what the Holy Spirit does.

Faithfulness   When you discover your spiritual gift and put it to work in a ministry, stick with it! God will bless your faithfulness.

Gentleness   Just because you have a spiritual gift doesn't give you license to barge into people's lives. Jesus was and is always a gentleman. The more confident we are in our spiritual gifts, the more often we need to remind ourselves to use our soft voices! Even in situations where you know you are right, be gentle. A word of wisdom, knowledge, discernment, or faith will almost certainly go unheeded unless it is delivered gently.

Self-Control   It is fitting that this is the last fruit. Paul taught in 1 Corinthians 14 that even the gift of tongues was subject to the control of the speaker. That is certainly true of all the other gifts as well. "The Holy Spirit made me do it" is no excuse for the untimely exercise of your spiritual gift, because He is the agent of self-control. Even when you feel compelled to go out of your way to exercise your gift, think about timing. If the timing is not God's timing, back off! God's gifts, used in God's way, in God's time–that's the formula for joy, energy, and effectiveness in the use of your spiritual gifts. May God bless you as you serve Him.

BIBLIOGRAPHY

Many books have been written on the subject of spiritual gifts. Some are theological. Some are practical. Some are written with a Pentecostal bias. Some are written with an anti-Pentecostal bias. The books in this list are primarily balanced in their perspective, practical in their presentation, and evangelical in their purpose. Each author has his or her own unique and interesting positions, but there are also a good deal of confirmation and agreement among them. (Note: Many may no longer be in print.)

Blanchard, Tim. *A Practical Guide to Finding and Using Your Spiritual Gifts.* Wheaton: Tyndale House, 1983.

Bryant, Charles V. *Rediscovering the Charismata.* Waco: Word, 1986.

Burns, Jim, and Doug Fields. *Congratulations, You Are Gifted!* Eugene: Harvest House, 1986. (A workbook written for students, it has wonderful illustrations of many of the gifts.)

Flynn, Leslie B. *19 Gifts of the Spirit.* Wheaton: Victor, 1974 (A classic that tackled this issue early—and clearly.)

Gangel, Kenneth O. *Unwrap Your Spiritual Gifts.* Wheaton: Victor, 1983. (Well organized and readable treatment from this Dallas Seminary scholar.)

Gilbert, Larry. *Team Ministry: A Guide to Spiritual Gifts and Lay Involvement.* Lynchburg: Church Growth Institute, 1987.

Hubbard, David. *Unwrapping Your spiritual Gifts.* Waco: Word, 1985.
(Another solid classic.)

Joiner, Barbara. *Yours for the Giving: Spiritual Gifts.* Birmingham: WMU, 1986.
(An interesting treatment written primarily for women.)

Jones, R. Wayne. *Using Spiritual Gifts.* Nashville: Broadman, 1985.
(Written from the perspective of a minister of education.)

MacGorman, J. W. *The Gifts of the Spirit.* Nashville: Broadman, 1980.
(A thorough treatment of the subject from the perspective of biblical
theology.)

McCrae, William J. *The Dynamics of Spiritual Gifts.* Grand Rapids: Zondervan,
1976.

Miller, Michael. *Ministry Gifts Inventory.* Nashville: Convention, 1995. (This
inexpensive booklet, offering a gifts inventory and scoring sheet, was designed
to help individuals, groups, and entire congregations discover their spiritual
gifts.)

Wagner, C. Peter. *Your Spiritual Gifts Can Help Your Church Grow.* Ventura:
Regal, 1982. (The book that got me interested in this subject. Required
reading for a course in church evangelism at Southwestern Seminary taught
by Dr. Roy Fish.)

Yohn, Rick. *Discover Your Spiritual Gift and Use It.* Wheaton: Tyndale, 1982.

Ideas for Leading Weekly Group Discussions

The leader guide on the following pages includes:
- Group-leader ideas
- Weekly group-session plans

Read every section before you plan for your group's sessions.

Group-Leader Ideas

Who? A group study of *Spiritual Gifts: A Practical Guide to How God Works Through You* is appropriate for any discipleship, prayer, or small group, as well as one-to-one discipling. The study will benefit adult believers of all ages.

When? Meet at a time and place appropriate for your group. Sessions can be conducted within 50 to 60 minutes. Group plans in this section serve as a framework; your goal should be to meet the learning needs of those in your group.

How? Use the weekly group session plans. Before each session, as group leader you should—
- pray for each group member;
- complete and prepare material for that week;
- encourage each group member;
- contact those who missed the previous session.

God bless you as you allow Him to direct you.

Session 1: An Introduction to Spiritual Gifts

1. Giving and receiving gifts is always a time of celebration. For each session make the room festive and inviting. Arrive early to ensure that the room is in order. Remove materials—curriculum, items on the wall, record books, forms, and other items—that will not be used for this study.

2. Have several small tables set up. On each table will be several small gift bags. Use solid color bags, so that each table has the same three bags. Plan to use these bags every week. This week one bag will contain name tags. Another will contain markers. And a third gift bag will contain a puzzle that can be worked fairly quickly. Before placing the puzzle in the bag, remove one or more pieces. Remove inside pieces rather than pieces that form the edge of the puzzle so that it will take longer to discover they are missing. Place missing pieces from each puzzle in a separate envelope and label it so you can give the missing pieces to each group later on. Plan to use the gift bags later for small gifts at the end of this and every session.

3. Prepare a marker board, chalkboard, or flipchart for use during the session. Plan to have it in place for every session. List Scripture passages you will be using. Also list the Greek words discussed in week 1.

4. As participants arrive, direct them to a table. Instruct them to introduce themselves to one another, make name tags, and begin to work on the puzzle.

5. After everyone arrives, allow a few minutes for them to complete the puzzle. Share their frustration at the missing pieces, but offer no explanation.

6. Welcome everyone to the study. Express your joy and enthusiasm. Affirm participants for wanting to know more about spiritual gifts. Encourage participants to work through the study on their own so that they can contribute to group work and gain greater insights from one another.

7. Say: "This first week is an introduction to spiritual gifts. We want to ask and answer the questions that begin any new investigation: who, what, when, where, what, and why."

8. Depending on the size of your group, divide into two or more small groups. Groups can easily be formed by those who worked in puzzle teams together. Each team will answer the assigned question(s). In their response to present to the larger group, they will include relevant Scripture references and word studies. Questions include:

    • Who has spiritual gifts?
    • Who gives the gifts?

- When and where are they to be used?
- What are the gifts?
- Why were they given?

Allow the groups time to prepare answers and report. As groups report, affirm, clarify, and be prepared to add to their comments as needed.

9. Say: "In this week's study we have learned that everyone has gifts and that a church shows a complete picture of Christ and the totality of gifts. Sometimes it is easier to see gifts in another than in yourself. When you are asked to serve in a church role, it is often because someone has seen gifts needed for that role in you."

10. Direct attention to the descriptions of gifts in day 3. Tell the group to think about who in the church has these gifts. Read a description and let the group respond. This is not a time to try to name all members of this group or to make anyone uncomfortable. If no one can think of a person with a particular gift, note that gift and at the end of this activity, pray that God will send people with those gifts to your church or reveal those gifts in current members so that your church will reflect Him completely.

11. Give each group the missing puzzle pieces to complete their work. Say: "Just as every puzzle piece is important to complete the picture, every person in a church is gifted and important in showing a complete image of God."

12. Dismiss the group with this prayer: "Lord, You have called us to be Your servant people. Grant that we may dwell in Your presence and love one another. In the name of Jesus Christ, amen."

13. As participants leave, give each a puzzle piece. Tell them to place it with their study materials to remind them of their important role in completing the big picture of your church.

Session 2: Gifts That Get Things Done

1. In advance enlist a church-staff minister or lay leader with gifts of leadership or administration to address the group. He should prepare to speak for no more than 10 minutes. Ask the speaker to tell how he discovered his gifts, how he has used them, how using them is fulfilling, how others are needed to complement the work he does.

2. Using the same room arrangement with tables and chairs and gift bags as the centerpiece, prepare these items for the gift bags.
- In one bag on each table place a plastic bag with at least a dozen sugar cubes, a blindfold, and these instructions:

Take turns assuming these roles: (1) One person is to be blindfolded. This person will have 30 seconds to stack as many sugar cubes as possible. (2) This person will coach the one stacking the sugar cubes. (3) Other players observe but do not speak.

- In a second gift bag place a plastic bag with 17 toothpicks and in a second plastic bag place 10 gumdrops. Include these instructions:
  Read instructions without speaking. No one is to lead. Everyone must participate. The goal is to build a house, using all the materials.

3. As participants arrive, welcome them and direct them to a table. Each table will need at least three participants. When at least three have arrived at a table, ask them to begin working on the project with the toothpicks and gumdrops. All should be in the same color bag so that you can say, "When three people have arrived, begin work on the blue bag." After all tables have completed this project, ask them to begin on the other one.

4. Around the tables, ask small groups to discuss: "In the first activity were you frustrated that no one was assigned a leadership role? Were you frustrated that you could not speak? Did someone, even without speaking, take charge of the task?" Then discuss the second project: "Which role was most comfortable?"

5. Introduce this week's topic, "Gifts That Get Things Done." Introduce the guest speaker.

6. After the presentation allow a few questions.

7. Tell the group that biblical examples of persons having these gifts include Moses, Nehemiah, and Jesus. Provide Bibles and commentaries, and other resource books. Divide into three small groups to prepare reports on these three men. Each report should include evidence of the gift, how it was used, and how that gift influenced or included others.

8. Lead a brief discussion on the difference in having a gift and the responsibility of all Christians. The content from this week's study on giving provides a model. Ask the group to point out other areas that similarly are the responsibility of all Christians but areas in which some have special gifts (evangelism, leadership, for example).

9. Close in prayer, thanking God for the gifts that get things done. Pray that God will call and use leaders with these gifts in your church and that others will support and affirm those with these gifts.

10. As participants leave, give each an individually wrapped candy orange slice to enjoy as they recall this week's study.

Session 3: Gifts That Engage Persons Outside the Church

1. Enlist some people with the gift of hospitality to help you with this session. They may or may not be involved in this study. Ask them to provide light refreshments and to greet and serve people as they arrive.
2. After people are served, direct them to take their refreshments to one of the tables. Once several people have gathered at a table, instruct them to take turns pulling a slip of paper out of a bag and to follow the instructions or answer the question. Then return the paper to the bag. Several people may answer the same question. Use these questions:

   - Tell about your own salvation experience. Who led you to Christ or encouraged you to become a Christian?
   - Tell about an experience when someone showed hospitality to you. How did that experience make you feel?
   - Tell about someone you know who has the gift of mercy. This person may be involved in a church project or in an agency or activity outside the church.
   - Name a person in your church who has a gift that engages persons. Explain your reason for choosing this person.

3. After everyone has arrived and had time to fellowship and talk about their topics, thank those who helped provide refreshments and hospitality for evening.
4. In advance enlist a church-staff minister, a missionary, or a lay leader with gifts of evangelism or apostleship to address the group. He should prepare to speak for no more than 10 minutes. Ask the speaker to tell how he discovered his gifts, how he has used them, how using them is fulfilling, how others are needed to complement the work he does. Allow a few minutes for questions.
5. Turn the discussion to the role that all Christians have in the gifts. Discuss the gifts studied this week and the ways all Christians are responsible for those gifts. Engage participants in this discussion by asking for examples and illustrations. Option: Prepare a story about the life of a missionary or tell about a contemporary missionary you read about in a publication from the International or North American Mission Boards or another mission organization.
6. In advance enlist a church-staff minister or lay leader who is active in the church's evangelism or outreach ministry. He should prepare to speak for

no more than 10 minutes, telling people how they can be involved in this ministry. Option: Get a video or print resource from the mission boards and tell about ways participants can be involved.

7. If your church has evangelism resources such as *Share Jesus Without Fear* or *Life on Mission,* show those to the group and encourage them to get involved in private or group study.

8. Discuss the thought from this week's study that more people discover their gift by trying different roles in the church than by reading about the gift or taking a test. Encourage everyone to get involved in ministries to discover whether they have gifts that engage persons.

9. Close in prayer thanking God for members with these gifts.

10. As people leave, give them a copy of a soul-winning tract. Encourage them to read it often and to watch for opportunities to share Christ with others.

Session 4: Gifts That Ground Us in God's Word

1. Arrange the room for a panel discussion, with chairs or tables and chairs across one end of the room.

2. At each small group table have enough hymnals for each person to have one. As participants arrive, direct them to a table. Invite them to find a favorite hymn and talk about it with table mates.

3. After everyone has arrived, welcome them and introduce this week's topic, "Gifts That Ground Us in God's Word."

4. Introduce the panel you have preenlisted of people in the church who have a variety of gifts in this area—teachers of various age groups, leaders of various groups such as missions education organizations and men's and women's ministries, and others. Ask each to speak briefly about what they do and how they find fulfillment and joy in that role. After all have spoken, invite questions.

5. In a gift bag on each table have these items: pens or pencils, paper, a sheet of large paper at least 11 by 17, and a felt-tip marker. Assign each table one of these: prophet, exhorter, teacher, or shepherd. Instruct them to use their Bible study books, their Bibles, and their creativity to write a job description for the role assigned to their group. The job description should include required and desired skills, gifts, and benefits. Encourage them to have fun.

6. Let someone from each group share the job description and display it on the wall. (Be sure to have masking tape available.)

7. Invite a few people to tell about their favorite hymns. Sing a verse of some familiar hymns.

8. Close in prayer, thanking God for gifting people in your congregation with gifts that ground people in God's Word.
9. As each person leaves, let him or her choose a bookmark from the gift bag. The bookmark should have a verse of Scripture on it to remind the participant of these gifts.

Session 5: Supplemental Gifts

1. You will need three small groups for this week's session. For each table line a gift bag with plastic and fill it with snack mix for people to enjoy while they work on their assignments.
2. Begin with a debate about the theological positions of the gifts in this section. Assign one of the three positions in the introduction to week 5 to each of the groups. Provide Bibles, commentaries, pencils or pens, and paper so that participants may begin to research and prepare as soon as they arrive.
3. When everyone has arrived, welcome them and announce that a great theological debate is about to take place. Set the stage by making this fun. The goal is not to have a winner but to share insights from different perspectives. Each group will get three minutes to present their case. After each group has presented the first time, each gets another two minutes to summarize their points.
4. After the debate summarize using points from the discussion about Pentecost in day 1 and the section about the gift of wisdom as supplemental to Scripture in day 2.
5. Ask participants to remain in their small groups to prepare reports to share with the group.

> Group 1: Knowledge and Wisdom
> Group 2: Faith and Discernment
> Group 3: Macro, Micro, and Mix

Each group will summarize the content in the lessons, using Scripture and personal illustrations or illustrations that relate to your church.
6. After each group has shared their report, ask members to review their notes for the past five weeks and to find a Scripture that has become important to them in this study. Allow a few minutes for them to review and select a Scripture.

7. Invite volunteers to share their verse and why they chose it. After all have shared who choose to share, close in prayer, thanking God for uniquely gifting this group and your church.
8. As participants leave, from the gift bag, give each a plastic zip bag of the snack mix.

Session 6: Gifts That Engage Persons Outside the Church

1. If you have not already done so, plan for participants to take a gifts inventory when they arrive. If you have already done this, invite them to review their inventory and to talk with the group at their table about it.
2. As people arrive, play choral music with multiple parts.
3. Either lead discussions or invite two guests in advance to present minilectures on (1) gifts and the fruit of the Spirit and (2) the along-the-way and out-of-the-way principle.
4. Invite representatives from as many different areas of work in your church as possible to attend. More than one from an organization should attend if possible. If possible there should be a ministry leader/worker for every two or three study participants. Ask one leader from each area to describe briefly the kinds of opportunities for putting gifts to work that are available in that area of ministry. In advance provide these leaders with the charts from this chapter about opportunities for service in the church. Ask leaders to prepare handouts about their organizations, opportunities for service, and whom people can contact if interested in serving.
5. After the brief presentation, plan a time of celebration for leaders to talk with participants about their organizations. Encourage leaders in advance to have ways participants can get involved right away by observing, partnering with an existing leader, getting training, or in some other way. Set a time limit for this part of the session.
6. Ask members to stand in a circle. Read the memory verse for the week, Romans 12:4-5. Invite volunteers to offer sentence prayers, seeking God's leadership in discovering and using gifts, thanking God for gifts, thanking Him for a place to serve.
7. Encourage those who still want to talk to do so or to set up a time to continue their discussions.
8. Give each person a helium-filled balloon to celebrate being gifted by God, discovering those gifts, and finding ways to use those gifts in ministry.